THE
5
SECRETS
OF
TEEN
SUCCESS

THE
CODE

THE
5
SECRETS
OF
TEEN
SUCCESS

Mawi Asgedom

Megan Tingley Books
LITTLE, BROWN AND COMPANY
New York · An AOL Time Warner Company

Also by Mawi Asgedom:

OF BEETLES AND ANGELS

First Edition

ISBN 0-316-82633-2 hardcover
ISBN 0-316-73689-9 paperback

10 9 8 7 6 5 4 3 2 1

Book design by Saho Fujii

Q-FF

Printed in the United States of America

The text was set in Formata Light, and the display type is Eraser Dust.

To my brother Tewolde

— *May* The Code *inspire others
half as much as you inspire me.*

CONTENTS

AUTHOR WARNING

The Code may cause some or all of the following effects:

- Anxiety resulting from too many dating opportunities
- Nausea caused by a sudden rise in grade point average
- Fever due to increased warmth from friends and family
- Confusion caused by piles of college acceptance letters
- Dizziness resulting from skyrocketing self-confidence

PROCEED WITH CAUTION!

As soon as I had finished my speech, I saw them moving toward me. A teenage boy, head bowed, like a prisoner being marched to jail. Behind him, his mother, pushing him forward. Since their school's assembly had just ended, other students lingered nearby.

The mother, brimming with confidence, grabbed my hand and shared her problem.

"Mawi," she said, "I told my son that he shouldn't dye his hair. He should have enough self-confidence based on how he is naturally. But he keeps arguing with me. Can you tell him that he doesn't need to change to stand out?"

Dang! Either the son or the mom was gonna be mad at me!

"I hear you," I told her. "Self-confidence is definitely the number one thing a teenager needs, and I'm glad you're teaching your son to value himself.

"To be honest with you, though," I continued, "I think he can have self-esteem *with* dyed hair. I never dyed my hair, but I used to let my friends shave designs into the back of my head, and we had a blast with it.

"Since you're the parent, it's your decision. But my honest opinion is that you should let him do it. Show him that he's cool, with or without dyed hair, and that you'll always support him for what's inside him."

The mom's jaw dropped halfway to the floor. She'd been sure I would side with her just because she was the parent.

But that's not what I'm about. And that's not what this book is about. This book isn't about taking sides between parents and teenagers. It's not about preaching old-fashioned messages.

It's about being honest. I promise you that in this book, I'll be honest. I'll be straight-up. I'll tell you what I think, and I won't water it down, because I'm not writing it to satisfy any particular reader. I'm writing it because I want to give you knowledge that can change your life.

Before I go any further, though, let me introduce my-self and explain how I learned about success.

Who Am I?

My name is Selamawi Haileab Asgedom — Mawi, for short — and I shouldn't even be around to write this book. I should have died a long time ago — eaten by a hyena, killed by black fever, or blown up by a rebel group. But I wasn't killed. I've made it to age twenty-six and feel blessed to be here now.

I was born half a world away in Ethiopia, in a small town called Adi Wahla. I'd have grown up in Adi Wahla, except for one problem: Ethiopia was in the midst of a thirty-year civil war with its northern region, Eritrea. Unfortunately for my family, our village was located right on the Ethiopian-Eritrean border.

Men from our village fled the brutal armies, and one day, my father fled as well. He walked hundreds of miles to Sudan, leaving the rest of us in Ethiopia. Six months later, my mother took my five-year-old brother Tewolde, my baby sister Mehret, and me on the long trek to meet up with my dad. I was three years old.

Along the way, some of our friends were eaten by hyenas. Others were kidnapped and sold into slavery. Still others died from sickness or hunger or thirst.

My family was fortunate to reach Sudan safely. We found my father and settled in a refugee camp. After three years in the camp, our lives changed forever: We moved across the world to Wheaton, Illinois, a town just outside Chicago.

Was the transition to America easy? Not for a minute. I had to learn a new language, get by on welfare, and make friends in a town where I was different from everyone else. Time after time, I wanted to give up: when bullies picked on me; when my school threatened to expel me for fighting; and even in high school, when a drunk driver killed my best friend, my brother Tewolde.

But I kept going, and by using the Secrets you'll find in this book, I eventually earned a full-tuition scholarship to Harvard University.

Now that I've graduated, I work as a professional speaker. I travel all over the country, showing students how to succeed.

By "succeed," I don't just mean getting into a famous college or becoming an all-state athlete. I'm talking about real success — being comfortable with who you are, choosing your own goals, and making yourself the person you've always known you could be.

The 5 Secrets

Working as a professional speaker, I've met every kind of teenager there is: confident and insecure, happy and miserable, overachieving and underperforming.

I've spoken in middle schools and high schools, in expensive private schools and old, rundown schools. I've even spoken with teens in jail. Wherever I've gone, I've always asked myself: what makes these teenagers who they are? What qualities separate the teens who are happy from the ones who aren't?

I finally found my answer: The 5 Secrets of Teen

Success. The 5 Secrets can make a weak teenager strong and turn a class geek into a class leader. They won't change your life overnight, but if you keep applying them, they can make you anything you want to be.

While you'll have to read this book to learn what each Secret means, for now I'll reveal their names:

THE 1ST SECRET: WIN THE INNER BATTLE
THE 2ND SECRET: WIN EVERY DAY
THE 3RD SECRET: GIVE FIRST, RECEIVE SECOND
THE 4TH SECRET: NEVER LOSE HOPE
THE 5TH SECRET: TAKE SMART RISKS

The 1st Secret will introduce you to The Code and help you create your own Code. The other 4 Secrets will help you live your Code.

You're probably wondering what The Code is and why it's important. You'll know in a few pages, but for now, I can tell you that *you* are The Code and The Code is you. That may sound strange, but I promise you: The Code has tremendous power. Used properly, it can change your life.

The Last Word

Over these past couple of years, I've read dozens of books on success. While many of those books offer useful information, most suffer from one problem: they're so long, it's hard to keep the lessons straight. By the time you get to page 200, you've forgotten what you learned on page 30. To avoid that, I've kept my book short and to the point.

I've also packed my book with captivating stories. Each one illustrates a strategy for success. I hope you'll like the stories, but I need to warn you: The stories alone won't make you succeed. To see why, think back to when you were a little kid. You learned how to ride a bike. Did you learn by hearing stories about biking? By watching your friends bike?

No. Watching and asking questions might have prepared you for riding a bike, but in the end, the only way you learned was by getting on the bike and finding out for yourself.

Success is the same way. I can tell you how others

have succeeded or how I've succeeded. But in the end, I can't make you succeed. If you want to succeed, you have to hop on the bike of success yourself, and make the wheels turn by applying the knowledge I give you.

To help you, I've closed each chapter with a section called "Your Turn," where you'll find questions that will help you unlock your potential. If you're serious about success, get a pen and some paper, and answer every question you find in "Your Turn."

And if you're ready to discover The Code and The 5 Secrets, turn the page.

THE 1ST SECRET:

Win the Inner Battle

To succeed on the outside — in activities, school, and your relationships with other people — you first have to succeed on the inside by taking control of your mind.

The 1st Secret is the foundation for all success and the most powerful thing I can teach you. It is divided into three sections:

- PRESS YOUR LIFE TURBO BUTTON
- START WITH YOUR HEART
- CHOOSE YOUR OWN DIRECTION

PRESS YOUR LIFE TURBO BUTTON

A couple of years ago, my little brother Hntsa (HINT-sa) and I were playing Nintendo basketball, and he was schooling me. Dunking on me. Running circles around me.

I couldn't believe it. It was one thing to lose, but he was destroying me. Game after game, no matter what I did, I couldn't come close.

I started to practice in secret. No way my little bro was gonna do me like that. I hooked up the Nintendo when he wasn't looking and played for hours. I'll surprise him, I thought. I'll practice, then whip him.

We played again, and he smoked me again. And again and again and again.

Finally, I asked him: "Hntsa, how come you're always killing me, man? What's going on?"

Hntsa turned his joystick upside down and showed

me a button I didn't realize existed. It was the turbo button. It made you jump higher, run faster, block harder. No wonder he was smoking me. No matter what I did, there was no way that I could compete with him: I didn't have my turbo button pressed.

Playing video games with Hntsa reminded me of a turbo button I had discovered in life, a secret button that can launch anyone to spectacular success. Like the turbo button on the Nintendo joystick, the life turbo button is hard to find unless you know where to look. You won't find it in school, sports, friends, or music. It's so close, it's hard to see.

Where does the life turbo button lie? Inside your mind. Next to the button, a label reads: PRESS IF YOU WANT TO TAKE ACTION TO IMPROVE YOUR LIFE. Very few people have pressed this button, but it's not hard to spot those who have.

What separates them? The turbo folks are always taking action to improve their lives. The folks who haven't pressed their turbo button, well, they're always making excuses about something.

You know the type: They always blame bad grades on their teachers or whine about how their parents aren't cool. You might hear them say:

"It's not fair my coach hates me. He's the only reason I'm not starting."

"I hate my body. How come I can't look better?"

"My parents pick on me all the time. I wish they'd just see things my way."

"I can't do well because someone else is preventing me. I don't have any power to improve my life, so I'll just complain about it."

Compare those complaints with the words of people who've pressed their life turbo button:

"I'm gonna talk to my coach and find out what it

would take for me to start. Then I'm gonna do my best to make it happen."

"I will make myself the most attractive person I can be. I don't have to look like a model — as long as I take care of myself, I'll be happy with my appearance."

"My parents don't always understand where I'm coming from, but I'm not going to let that ruin our relationship. I will talk to them, respect them, and try to see things their way, and hopefully they'll respond by doing the same for me."

"I know I can't control everything in my life, but I still believe that it's up to me to create the life I want. I will make things happen for myself through my own effort."

Which group of people has a better chance of succeeding? Which type of person do you want to be?

The Original Turbo Brother

When we first came to America, my older brother Tewolde, my sister Mehret, and I saw other kids in our neighborhood riding their bikes. Naturally, we wanted bikes too. But our family was barely scraping by on welfare, so our parents couldn't buy them for us.

What did Tewolde do? Instead of complaining or just accepting that we couldn't have bikes, he asked himself the turbo question: *What action can I take to improve my situation?*

Tewolde started scouting around local Dumpsters. Before long, he found one bike that had a front tire he could use. Then he found another bike with a good frame and back tire. Then another bike that had a seat he liked. Tewolde combined the parts and put together a whole bike.

When he was done, he helped my sister and me assemble our own bikes. We went from no bike to three bikes, from watching our friends bike to biking with them. How? By pressing the turbo button.

Years later, Tewolde used his turbo button again. He was a junior in high school, needed money for college, and wanted to help my parents with the bills. Tewolde asked himself: *What can I do to make more money?*

Notice that Tewolde didn't ask: *How come most of the families in Wheaton have money, and mine is on Welfare?* Or: *Why is college so expensive?* Or: *Why won't someone else help me out?* No, he asked himself the turbo question: ***What action can I take to improve my situation?***

One day, while working his job as a janitor, Tewolde noticed something funny: The building owner paid Tewolde's boss $35 an hour, but as an employee, Tewolde got only $7 an hour.

If he became his own boss, Tewolde figured, he could start making $35 an hour. So at age sixteen, he pressed his turbo button and decided to start Pro Clean, Inc.

No one would hire Tewolde at first because they hadn't heard of his company. But he refused to quit. He posted flyers and asked his friends to spread the word. Before long, he had one customer, then two, then three.

PRO CLEAN
NO ONE CLEANS BETTER

TEWOLDE ASGEDOM

Soon he started banking $35 an hour on a regular basis. He had quintupled his income.

Do you see the power of the turbo button? It's $35 in your pocket instead of $7. Three bikes instead of none. Pressing your life turbo button can take you from C's to A's, from loneliness to having friends, from sitting on the bench to starting for your sports team.

Want to know the best part? Pressing your life turbo button is as easy as pressing a button on a joystick. Anyone can do it. All you have to do is sincerely believe:

I realize that no one — not my parents, friends, school, government, no one — can make me suc-ceed. Others can help, but ultimately, I will succeed only when I take responsibility for everything that I can control: how I think, how I talk, how hard I work, how I treat others — all my actions. Complaining about life won't get me anywhere. Instead, I'm al-ways going to focus on the actions I can take to improve my life.

☛ YOUR TURN: PRESS YOUR LIFE TURBO BUTTON

People who haven't pressed their turbo button look at things they don't like in their lives and say, "There's nothing I can do about it." Those who *have* pressed their turbo button believe they can take steps to improve any area of their life.

❶ What would you like to improve in your life? You can pick from any number of things: friendships, athletic performance, appearance, family relationships, grades, money — you name it. Write down a list of ideas and choose the three that are most important to you.

❷ For each improvement opportunity you chose, write down the specific things you would have to do to make it happen. If you want to raise your D average to a B, you might write down: "I must go to class every day, turn in every assignment, study for every test, and ask my teachers for extra-credit projects."

❸ To give yourself motivation, write why you want to make each change. Will it make you feel better? Will it make you or your family more proud? Will it give you more opportunities in life? Write down as many reasons as you can. Read and reread these explanations whenever you need inspiration.

❹ Don't wait until tomorrow. Take action on at least one of your improvement opportunities today. If you said you want to get good grades, do your homework right now. If you want to learn guitar, start looking for a guitar. Take action to improve your life.

START WITH YOUR HEART

When my family lived in a refugee camp in Sudan, we didn't have access to a grocery store. Because we needed fruits and vegetables to survive, we planted some corn next to our straw-and-mud adobe.

One day, my father asked me — little six-year-old Mawi — to water our family garden. So I picked up our big wooden bucket, walked past the other adobes, and filled the bucket at the village well.

My bucket full, I stumbled over to the first plant and, starting from the top, sprinkled just enough water to cover the nearest ear of corn. Once the ear was wet, I kneeled and splashed the stalk. Then I moved to the next ear and started again.

About halfway through, I bumped into my father, who — try as he might — couldn't hide his smile. He looked down at me and, in his booming voice, told me something I'll never forget:

> YOU GAVE DRINK TO THE STALK AND THE EARS OF CORN BECAUSE YOU CAN SEE THEM AND THEY LOOK LIKE THEY ARE THE MOST IMPORTANT PART OF THE PLANT. BUT DEEP BELOW THE GROUND, FAR FROM SIGHT, YOU WILL FIND THE TRUE HEART OF THIS PLANT: THE ROOT. YOU CAN WATER THE OUTER STALK ALL DAY LONG, BUT IF YOU HAVEN'T WATERED THE ROOT, THE ENTIRE STALK WILL DIE.

We can learn quite a bit from my innocent mistake. Just as I was drawn to the obvious — watering the outer stalks — you may be tempted to pursue promising outer goals, such as attending a prestigious college or being popular at school. But the truth is, you'll experience lasting happiness only if you start with what's inside you.

That's why when you look for ways to press your turbo button, you should look to your heart. If you start by examining your beliefs and character, you'll be watering your roots, and everything else in your life will grow naturally: friendships, college admissions, academic and athletic success.

Proud to Be Me

If you want to know how strong your heart is, ask yourself one question: *Am I proud to be me?* I know I wasn't always proud to be Mawi Asgedom.

When I was a kid, my teachers used to send forms home, asking parents to sign up for conference times. I never let my parents see those forms — I always ripped them up so my parents wouldn't set foot in my school.

My dad had visited our elementary school once, and for years after, I remembered the stares. He had shouted in broken English, twice as loud as everyone else, and dressed even worse than I did — an amazing feat, trust me. I didn't want my mother coming either, because she barely spoke English and I always had to translate for her.

But by the time I got to high school, I realized that my parents, culture, and background were an important part of who I was — even if they made me different. As I became less dependent on what my classmates thought of me, I got to the point where I could tell anyone: *"These are my parents. They're on welfare. They don't speak English. They're probably not as cool as your parents. But guess what: I love them. I'm proud of them. And I don't care what any of y'all think."*

Once I embraced the fact that I was different, I transformed myself into a new person. I didn't have to change to make myself fit in. I didn't have to be as good-looking or athletic or funny as everyone else. I just had to be me.

And the cool part is, once I became proud of my culture, people suddenly wanted to learn about it. They wanted me to take them to Ethiopian restaurants and show them Ethiopian dancing. Being different actually became a huge advantage.

How about you? You may try your hardest to fit in, but the truth of the matter is, you'll never be able to fit in 100 percent of the way. So why fight the fact that you're different?

Instead of trying to fit everyone else's definition of

cool, you can choose a better option: Look inside your heart and decide that you're cool, no matter what anyone thinks. Be proud of your differences, and make them work for you instead of against you.

Beliefs Are the Foundation

If you accept yourself, you'll live with much greater confidence. And you'll be ready to take control of another part of your heart: your personal beliefs. How important are your beliefs? More important than *anything*.

To see why, just think about the impact your beliefs have. What if you believed that you were dumb and that you could never succeed — or even that good grades were just for nerds. Would you ever try hard at school? No way. With beliefs like those, you'd have no reason to try.

What if the opposite were true and you held empowering beliefs? Say you were *certain* that the guy or girl you liked would go out with you. Would you ask them out? Sure. Since you believed that you could get the date, you would try to make it happen.

23

Beliefs even control such simple, everyday activities as walking. For example, when you're crossing the street, you don't think twice about putting your foot on the ground. You believe, based on lots of experience, that the ground offers a solid foundation.

Let's say instead, though, that you believed the road in front of you were quicksand, not solid ground. Would you still try to cross the street? No way! You'd be too afraid to move forward, no matter how badly you wanted to reach the other side.

In the same way, if you believe that you can't succeed — in school, activities, making friends — you won't even try. Without the foundation of positive beliefs, succeeding would be impossible, like walking in quicksand.

But if you believe in yourself — believe you *can* succeed — you have the foundation you need to make it. You can take that step and try your hardest to succeed.

That's why Henry Ford's old saying is true: *Whether you believe you can or believe you can't, you're probably right.*

Discover Your Beliefs

You may not realize it, but you have many important personal beliefs inscribed in your heart. I don't mean religious beliefs. I'm talking about *everything* that you hold to be true.

Depending on who you are, your heart might tell you some of these things:

I am beautiful.	I am dumb.	I am lazy.
I am ugly.	I am honest.	I am a loser.
I am smart.	I am hardworking.	I am cool.

For a long time, I believed I wasn't cool. Why? Because my classmates told me: "You're different." "You're poor." "You're ugly." "You're a nerd and you're not cool." I allowed my classmates to dictate my beliefs, and I walked around with my head down.

But eventually, I realized that I was living in mental slavery. I realized that I was letting others control my life.

I saw that only I could free myself. So I pressed my turbo button, descended into my heart, and took action to improve my life. I chose my own beliefs: *I am beautiful. I am athletic. I am successful. I am cool. Not because anyone else tells me I am, but because I dare to believe it in my heart.*

My classmates still made fun of me. I still didn't have many friends. Things on the outside were far from perfect. But day by day, I kept doing my best to maintain positive beliefs about myself. And slowly, I felt myself growing more confident and more free.

Look at your own life. Who controls how you view yourself? You? Or everyone else around you?

If it's not you, now is the time to break free of your chains and choose your own personal beliefs. Now is the time to look the world in the eye and declare: *"FROM THIS DAY FORTH, YOU WILL NEVER AGAIN CONTROL MY BELIEFS. NO MATTER WHAT YOU SAY OR HOW YOU TRY TO INFLUENCE ME, I WILL ALWAYS MAINTAIN GREAT BELIEFS ABOUT MYSELF."*

☛ YOUR TURN: START WITH YOUR HEART

❶ Because they're not always easy to see, it can be hard to identify our beliefs. For the next couple of minutes, think really hard about who you are and try to identify your beliefs. Write down your beliefs, and if you don't like them, think about how you can change them.

❷ Are there any parts of yourself that you are ashamed of? What will you do in the future to feel more proud of yourself?

❸ If you want to change any of your beliefs, take the first step now: Write down what you used to believe, then put a line through it. Next to the old belief, write the new belief you've chosen.

CHOOSE YOUR OWN DIRECTION

For three days, my family had been stuck in a small Ethiopian village. Between us and Sudan lay miles of wilderness, filled with ferocious animals. My mother wanted to move on, and so did another refugee woman we knew.

"Come on, Tsege," she told my mother. "I'm anxious. Let's go."

But my mom wasn't sure we were ready. "I want to go," she said, "but first, let's make sure we're heading in the right direction. Let's find other travelers who will go with us and help us stay safe."

Despite my mother's urging, the woman refused to wait. She grabbed her things and rushed away. Several days later, they found her body — hyenas had devoured her. I'm sure glad my mom took time to think before she acted!

You and I are on a journey together — a success journey. Though our journey won't put us in physical danger, it won't be easy — nothing worthwhile in life is.

But if we do what my mother did — think about our journey's direction before we get started — we'll improve our chances of success. So let's pause to think carefully about where we want to go. Otherwise, we might find ourselves walking into life's hyenas.

The Ocean of Life

My family made it because my mother chose her own path instead of being swayed by the other woman. Know how you're going to succeed? That's right. By choosing your own path instead of blindly following others.

But choosing your own path isn't always easy. To see why, use your imagination and put yourself on a raft in the middle of the ocean. All around you, different currents are trying to pull you in different directions.

Your classmates might be one current. "If you wanna

be cool," they say, "you gotta dress a certain way, eat a certain way, and act a certain way." They're pushing you to become a certain kind of person.

Your parents are another current. They might say: "Think about your future." "Do your homework." "You're too young to date." "Don't hang out with bad people." They're pushing you to become another kind of person, different from what your friends want.

How about TV and movies? Doesn't pop culture constantly send you messages about what's cool and what's not?

You have a choice to make: Who will control how you think? Your friends? Your family? MTV? Or you?

Think you don't have to choose? That you can just go with the flow? Think again. If you follow life's currents and don't think about where you want to go, those currents — your friends, school, culture, and community — might sweep you under water or knock you off course.

Fortunately, you don't have to let others control where you end up in life. You can choose your own direction. You can become your own navigator on the ocean of life.

"I Don't Know Where to Go"

Everywhere I go, I encourage teenagers to choose their own direction. Most of the time, they look at me like I'm crazy. I know what they're thinking: *Mawi, I don't even know what I want to do this weekend — how am I gonna choose my life direction?*

I hear that. Even after I graduated from Harvard, I still didn't know what career I wanted to pursue.

But even if you don't know what you want on the outside — like what college you'll attend, whom you'll date, or what car you want to drive — you can always decide what kind of person you'll be on the inside.

You can choose whether you will be:

Lazy	or	Hardworking
Upbeat	or	Bitter
Confident	or	Insecure
Giving	or	Selfish
Kind	or	Rude

You can choose your attitude. You can make your own

rules: *I will not talk behind people's backs* or *I <u>will</u> talk behind people's backs.* And as we learned in the last section, you can choose your own beliefs instead of letting others choose your beliefs for you.

Want to know the best part? Choosing your inner direction is much more powerful than choosing your outer direction.

To see why, compare the inner character and outer goals of two teenagers, Jen and Monica:

Jen	Monica
Inner Character	*Inner Character*
Selfish	Generous
Lazy	Hardworking
Insecure	Confident
Mean	Friendly
Sneaky	Honest
Outer Goals	*Outer Goals*
Get a Scholarship	Don't Know Yet
Become a Great Athlete	Don't Know Yet
Have Lots of Friends	Don't Know Yet

Jen has great goals on the outside — she wants a scholarship, to become a great athlete, and to have lots of friends. But on the inside, she's selfish, sneaky, and mean. How is someone like that supposed to make friends? And if she doesn't work hard and is too insecure to believe in herself, what are her chances of earning a scholarship or succeeding in sports?

How about Monica? Even though she doesn't know her outer goals yet, she has decided to be generous, hardworking, and confident on the inside. Because she has great inner qualities, she'll probably succeed on the outside — with friends, in school, and with whatever other goals she decides to pursue.

So if you don't know all your outer goals yet, don't worry about it — few people do. Just make sure that you're headed in the right direction where it counts: on the inside. If you take care of your inner world — your attitude, beliefs, and character qualities — you're bound to do well on the outside.

Putting It All Together

We've talked about many powerful ideas in this chapter — direction, beliefs, turbo buttons, goals — and I know it may seem overwhelming.

There's no need to worry, though: It's about to come together.

In my introduction, I promised to explain The Code. I also promised that The Code had tremendous power — power that can change your life. What's The Code?

The Code is a tool you use to lead yourself — to control your beliefs, to achieve your goals, to become the person you want to be. It's a shield you use to protect your mind.

Creating your Code is easy: As my dad taught me when I watered the corn, you start with your heart. In the top of your Code, you write who you want to be on the inside: the beliefs you want to hold, the attitude you want to have — you might even give yourself some rules for navigating life's currents.

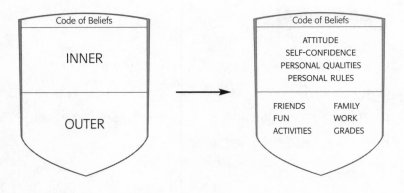

On the bottom half, you write your outer goals: what grades you want, whether you'd like to go to college, how you want to get along with friends and family, and any other big accomplishments you'd like to make.

Why is The Code so powerful? Because The Code helps you take the most important step in success: deciding who you will become. Instead of having others control your mind, you can write your own Code, choose your own direction, and become the person *you* want to be.

Take Control

In a moment, you'll have an opportunity to create your own Code. Before you dive in, though, you can learn from the Codes that three other teenagers have made. Be sure to look at each carefully:

Code of Beliefs

INNER

2 wrongs don't make a right

Keep trying because nothing is impossible

Don't sit around and be lazy, work till I'm tired

Creative — open-minded and have a different way of thinking

I always have high self-confidence

OUTER

School — I would like to go to college /
This quarter 3 A's 2 B's, 1 C

Activities: Wrestling — I will go at least 11-2 /
Must run 3 miles every day — stay in shape!

Personal: I want to find a girlfriend /
   Never be afraid to ask anyone out, go on a date
   every month

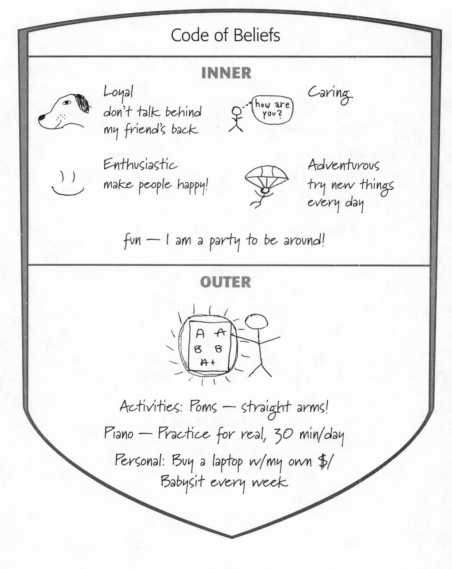

Code of Beliefs

INNER

Loyal
don't talk behind
my friend's back

Caring

Enthusiastic
make people happy!

Adventurous
try new things
every day

fun — I am a party to be around!

OUTER

Activities: Poms — straight arms!

Piano — Practice for real, 30 min/day

Personal: Buy a laptop w/my own $/
Babysit every week

Code of Beliefs

INNER

↑ I love God,
I live my faith

Outgoing — Let others
see more of who I am

Be kind — Don't make
anyone more upset
than they already are

Honest — keep my word
+ earn people's trust

Push my Turbo Button — I always take action
to make my life better

OUTER

School: Become a great writer. / read 50 pages
every week (not schoolwork), take Mrs. Jenkins'
fiction class.

Youth group: Always be upbeat and show
kindness to new people. / Talk to people who seem
left out each Sunday.

Family: Help mom more than usual. / Do
the laundry every Sunday.

Before these three teenagers could create their Codes, they had to invest time figuring out what they wanted and who they wanted to be. The same is ture for you. Creating a powerful Code will require you to think hard about who you want to be and where you want to go.

These next few pages will help you do just that — they'll help you create a powerful Code for yourself.

So ask yourself: Are you cool with having classmates, MTV, and the rest of the world run your life? If so, then don't worry about making your own Code — just skim through these pages. But if you want to step up and take control of your mind, then grab a pen and paper, take a few minutes, and follow these important steps:

START INSIDE

Since your inner beliefs drive your outer success, the way to start building a fantastic Code is to focus on your inner qualities first:

❶ BRAINSTORM: Get a piece of scratch paper and jot down any inner qualities you consider important, such as respect, hard work, honesty, loyalty, or courage (you don't have to use those — they're just ideas).

You might think about the people you admire in life and why you admire them. You can also write down quotes that inspire you, or, if you're a religious person, feel free to write about your faith. *Don't hold back — let your mind run free, and try to come up with at least ten inner qualities you value.* (If you need inspiration, turn to the back of this book, and you can find some of my favorite quotes.)

❷ PICK 5: Look at your list and pick the five personal qualities or beliefs that are most important to you — the five that define who you want to be. Why only five? If you pick too many, you might lose track of them all.

Once you've picked five, write a sentence describing what each one means to you. For example, you might write: "Generous — I give to those around me" or "Positive Attitude: I always choose to be positive — I don't complain."

41

❸ **Do it Your Way:** Take the five qualities you chose, and the descriptions you wrote about each, and put them in the top half of your Code diagram (p. 45). Since this is *your* Code, you can illustrate your qualities however you wish. You can write your beliefs as a list, draw them in a picture, turn them into a poem — whatever will motivate you to make them part of your life.

MOVE OUTSIDE

Although your inner beliefs are more important, outer goals will also help you — by giving you specific targets to shoot for and ways to focus your energy and time.

I know it's tough to come up with outer goals, so I'll give you a head start. Instead of trying to think of every goal you might want, just write down one goal for each of the three big categories: School, Activities, and Personal.

Your school goals might include your grades or

intended career; activities could relate to sports, clubs, or community groups; and personal might touch on your friends, family, health, or religion.

As you decide on your goals for each category, remember to:

❶ BE SPECIFIC: If your goals are general — you want good grades or want to get dates — you won't really know what you're aiming for.

But if you make your goals specific — "I want 3 A's and 3 B's this semester" or "I want to go on at least four cool dates this year" — you'll know exactly what you're aiming for and you'll have a better chance of hitting your target.

❷ GIVE YOURSELF DEADLINES: "I'll learn to play guitar someday." "I'll get good grades someday." "I'll learn to cook someday." Have you ever seen "someday" on a calendar?

The only way you'll make your goals a reality is if

43

you give them a deadline. So if you *really* want to learn how to play guitar, give yourself a clear time frame, such as, "I'll have bought a guitar <u>by the end of this month</u> and learned at least five chords <u>by the end of the semester</u>."

❸ SUPPORT YOUR LONG-TERM GOALS WITH SHORT-TERM GOALS: If one of your goals is having a band, then next to that goal you might write: "I'll practice every day during the next month and start looking for the other three band members."

By setting short-term goals that support your long-term goals, you start moving in the right direction right away.

Once you've decided on outer goals, you're ready for the moment of truth. Complete your Code by writing your goals in the bottom half: at least one goal each for school, activities, and your personal life.

My Code of Beliefs

I hope you realize the power of what you just did. By creating The Code, you've taken the most important step in success — choosing your own path.

Sure, you'll have to work on your Code some more to get a really good picture of who you want to be. But for now, you can take satisfaction in knowing that you've completed a huge first step.

Do you understand now what I meant in the introduction when I said, "*You* are The Code and The Code is you"? Your Code represents the real you: your goals, your attitude, your beliefs, and your dreams. By choosing your own Code, you're taking control of your life. You're Winning the Inner Battle.

☛ **YOUR TURN:** CHOOSE YOUR OWN DIRECTION

❶ I've often heard that the best way to learn something is to teach it to someone else. Find a friend, family member, or teacher, and show them how they can create their own Code. Walk them through the process that you used to come up with your Code.

❷ Pick a hero that you have — a family member, friend, or someone famous — and do your best to map out their Code. What kind of inner beliefs do you think that person maintains, and what do you think are their outer goals? On a separate piece of paper, draw a shield and fill in your impression of that person's Code.

THE 2ND SECRET:

Win Every Day

SINCE THE OUTSIDE WORLD WILL NEVER STOP TRYING TO CONTROL YOUR MIND, YOU CAN'T SETTLE FOR WINNING THE INNER BATTLE ONCE. YOU HAVE TO KEEP WINNING EVERY DAY.

Within this Secret, you'll learn just one lesson, but it's the key to living out your Code.

- **BE A TRUE LEADER**

BE A TRUE LEADER

Once you choose your Code, how do you think people will react? Will they leap to their feet and give you a standing ovation? Will your teachers snap their fingers and grant you A's? Will your classmates shower you with acceptance?

Maybe on *Sesame Street,* but not in the real world. In real life, you'll battle challenges and distractions. You might get sick, get cut from an activity, or face harassing classmates. Or you might fall victim to the most common trap: You might simply forget your Code and get swept away by life's currents.

Fortunately, you'll encounter some folks who'll help you live out your Code. But you'll also have to watch out for Spirit Crushers who'll try to bring you down.

Spirit Builders and Spirit Crushers

In high school, my friend Naomi had amazing beliefs. She was intelligent, sweet, funny, and fun to be around.

But her mom, who should have been her closest ally, was actually her biggest enemy. Instead of helping Naomi succeed, her mom abused her constantly — not by hitting her, but by calling her horrible names.

For a while, Naomi couldn't handle her mom's abuse. Naomi would spend weekends alone in her room, crying for hours on end.

But eventually, she made a turnaround. How? By turning to her Spirit Builders — people who supported her and built up her confidence.

Alone, Naomi had trouble overcoming her mom's negativity. But with an army of friends and teachers supporting her and complimenting her, Naomi found it easier to stay positive about her Code.

Think about your own life: Who are the Spirit Builders? Who are the Spirit Crushers? Are you a Spirit Builder for your friends and family?

The Power of Three

Rameck had spent time in jail for attempted murder. Sam for armed robbery. They were back in high school, but their futures looked bleak. Then their friend George told them about a speaker who had visited his science class. The speaker had shown George's class how any of them could attend college.

After thinking it over carefully, the three teenagers made a pact: They would work hard and earn admission to Seton Hall University, graduate, and go on to medical school.

All three came from single-parent homes and grew up in a violent neighborhood. There were many reasons why they shouldn't have made it.

But they did make it. For six years they helped each other study, stayed clear of trouble, and had fun together, too. They got scholarships to Seton Hall, attended medical school, and now, all three are doctors.

Their story illustrates the truth of the ancient proverb:

One strand of fabric snaps under pressure, but a cord of three strands is not easily broken.

If you want to make your Code a reality, find some folks whom you trust — whether they're adults or other teenagers — and share your Code with them. Ask them to help you live out your Code each day. And of course, ask whether they want help living out their Code.

The Lord of the Rings

If you choose the right friends, they'll help you reach your inner and outer goals. But your friends won't be able to do everything for you. At some point, *you* need to step up and strengthen yourself.

An example of this comes from my favorite book and movie trilogy, *The Lord of the Rings.* In the beginning of the books, one of the main characters, Aragorn, keeps to himself. He has tremendous power inside himself, but he doesn't even know it.

When the evil armies of Mordor threaten his people,

though, Aragorn realizes that he must act and must find others to help him. He makes friends who support him against Mordor.

But as Aragorn moves to confront Mordor, he finds that his army of supporters isn't enough. He needs a powerful weapon of his own — the ancient sword of his ancestors, who once defeated their dark foes.

In many ways, you're like Aragorn. You can assemble a powerful army of friends, family, teachers, and coaches who will help you overcome life's Spirit Crushers. You can turn to that army in times of trouble.

But if you want to reach your full potential, you can't rely just on your Spirit Builders. You'll need to turn inward and find your own special weapon, something that will give you extra strength as you defend your Code.

Journal Power

What's your secret weapon? It's something I discovered when I was fourteen.

One day after school, I got a blank notebook and turned it into my journal. In the front, I wrote what attitudes and beliefs I wanted to live out. I also chose my outer goals, like you did in your Code.

Each day, I wrote in my journal for a few minutes. Sometimes I wrote silly stuff, such as: "DANG! Sara looked GOOD today in gym class."

After the silly stuff, though, I always took a few minutes to check on my attitude and goals: "What direction am I flowing in as a person? How are my beliefs doing? Did I move toward my goals today?"

Sometimes I didn't like the answers. Sometimes I realized that I had let others control my level of my confidence, or that I had been lazy during basketball practice or mean to my family. Whenever that happened, I didn't get mad at myself. I just told myself that the next day I would try to be more confident, or work extra hard in practice, or be extra nice to my family.

Because I was taking time every day to lead myself, the rest of the world couldn't easily control me. I guided myself toward stronger beliefs and slowly felt my confidence grow. My classmates noticed, and little by little, they showed me more respect. More important, I was becoming the person I wanted to be.

Before long, guess who was asking about Mawi? That's right! Sara!

Be a True Leader

When most people talk about "leaders," they refer to people who have big titles, like the student-council president or the captain of a team. But true leadership isn't about being president or captain.

True leadership is about taking a few minutes each day to lead yourself toward your inner and outer goals. It's about reflecting on your life and making sure that you're headed in the right direction.

A personal journal is a great leadership tool because it helps you reflect on your life; it helps you Win your Inner Battle not just once, but *every day.* That's why of all the advice I give you in this book, this is the one piece I most hope you'll follow:

Get a journal. At the front, write what matters most: your Code.

Then, each day, look at your Code. Write for five minutes about your day and reflect on whether you made progress on your inner and outer goals. If you can't journal every day, try doing it once a week. ***You'll be amazed by the new power you feel.***

☞ YOUR TURN: BE A TRUE LEADER

❶ Make a drawing of yourself one year from now. Include how you're dressed, how you walk, who your friends are. Draw an army of Spirit Builders — if you know who you want in your army, give them names.

❷ What's on Your Wall?

You can give your heart encouragement by surrounding yourself with inspiring quotes, posters, and images.

If you walked into my apartment right now, you'd see plenty of inspiration: my brother Tewolde's card from his cleaning business. A framed quote from Nelson Mandela. Letters students wrote me after I spoke at their school. A basketball player slam-dunking.

Every time I see these quotes or images, I remember something about who I am, how I want to act, or what I believe in. I remind myself of all I want to accomplish.

What's on your wall? Are you surrounding yourself with greatness?

I challenge you to put up at least three inspiring images, quotes, or posters in your room or your locker. To get started, you can find some of my favorite quotes in the back of this book.

❸ Besides journaling, what are some other things that you could do to help yourself reflect on how you're living? (There's a different answer for everyone: Some people like talking to good friends or family; some like running and letting their mind wander; some like drawing.) See if you can figure out what will help you reflect on your progress.

THE 3RD SECRET:

Give First, Receive Second

WINNING THE INNER BATTLE WILL GIVE YOU TREMENDOUS INNER STRENGTH. BUT YOU'LL BE MUCH STRONGER — AND HAVE MORE FUN — IF YOU DEVELOP POSITIVE RELATIONSHIPS WITH FRIENDS, FAMILY, AND OTHER PEOPLE. THE 3RD SECRET WILL HELP YOU DEVELOP THOSE RELATIONSHIPS.

You'll find three ingredients to achieving this Secret:

- **NO THOUGHT OF REWARD**
- **SEE IT THEIR WAY**
- **GET IN THE GAME!**

NO THOUGHT OF REWARD

When we were kids, my brother Tewolde and I always looked forward to the weekend. Our father made us get up at 5:00 A.M. every weekday to exercise, so all we wanted to do Saturday morning was sleep late.

But our father, whom we called Babay, would have none of that. At the crack of dawn, his voice would echo all around our house.

"SELAMAWI, TEWOLDE, GET THE CLEANING BRUSHES," our father would order us. "IT'S TIME TO REMOVE THE LEAVES FROM THE DRIVEWAY."

This wasn't just any driveway — the driveway that separated our house from our neighbors' must have been 100 feet long. Raking it took hours, and if that weren't bad enough, we barely even used it — it really belonged to our neighbors.

Tewolde and I would protest with every possible argument: "Come on, Babay! It's early in the morning. It's cold outside. Our family uses only a small part of the driveway. No one expects us to rake the whole thing! Why can't our neighbors rake their own part?"

Our father's firm tone told us we had no choice.

"I KNOW YOU ARE MAD NOW, MY CHILDREN. BUT I AM TEACHING YOU HOW TO LIVE WELL WITH YOUR NEIGHBORS. YOU NEED TO LEARN, STARTING NOW, HOW TO GIVE TO OTHERS WITHOUT THOUGHT OF RE-WARD FOR YOURSELF."

For a long time, we thought our father was crazy. Who in their right mind woke up early on a Saturday morning to clear someone else's driveway for free?

But as we grew older, my brother Tewolde took our father's words to heart. Tewolde continued to rake the neighbors' leaves and also gave much more: He supported a homeless man who had no one else to turn to, gave to his classmates through kind words and actions, and even sent hundreds of dollars a year to support a child in South America — without telling anyone.

Years later, when Tewolde died, and again, when my

father passed away, I was stunned by the number of folks who came to honor their memories. The funeral-home directors said they had never witnessed such turnouts, not even for community leaders.

How was it that my brother and father — poor, black immigrants in a wealthy, white town — had meant something special to so many folks? *It was because they had given so much without expecting anything in return.*

See, most of us walk around thinking: *How can I make myself happy? What can I get? How can I get other people to hook me up?*

But what if we instead thought: *What can I give to those around me? How can I contribute to my school, to my family, to my friends, to my neighbors?*

Wouldn't we mean something special to other people? Wouldn't other people want to give back to us, too?

Just think about your own life. Whom do you value: the person who takes from you, or the person who gives to you?

If you give your school everything you have — hard work, a great attitude, respect for others — won't your teachers and counselors be more likely to appreciate you?

If you give your friends love, kindness, and support, won't they be more likely to give it back to you?

If you give your sports team effort, dedication, and a great attitude, won't your coaches more likely give you playing time? If you were the coach, wouldn't you want to give back to those who gave the most? I know I would.

So if you want to mean something special to others, don't just focus on what you can get. Start by focusing on what you can give — without expecting any reward.

Invisible Gifts

When we think of gifts we can give, we often think of money, clothes, or cool electronic gadgets. But sometimes, the greatest gifts are free.

After I graduated from college, I worked part time for a company called ShopTalk. At the same time, I was trying to start my inspirational-speaking business.

Speaking looked bleak. During the entire first year,

only seven people had hired me to speak, and they had paid me peanuts. I was ready to quit speaking and to work full time at ShopTalk.

Then my friend Corey McQuade invited me to speak at his old high school in Swanton, Ohio. The speech I gave at Corey's school outshone any I had given before. Two students liked it so much that they wrote about it in the local paper.

After the presentation, on the car ride back to Illinois, I told Corey that I was going to quit speaking. He couldn't believe it. "Don't do it, Mawi," he said. "You know what you really want. Have the courage to follow your dream. Don't quit speaking. Quit ShopTalk."

Corey didn't give me money that day. He didn't give me a car or a new computer. But he gave me gifts that were much more important: confidence and courage. I quit ShopTalk, focused on speaking, and now I speak to over 100,000 people each year.

See, offering money is just one way to give. Regardless of your financial wealth, you can always contribute gifts from your heart. You can make yourself a Spirit Builder for the people in your life.

You Give What You Have

Before you can give to others, though, your own heart has to be strong.

Let's say you want to give kindness to the kid that everyone else picks on.

If you're insecure in your own heart, will you help the unpopular kid? If you do, other people might pick on *you* — and that's a chance that no insecure person wants to take. If you're confident, though, you won't be concerned with what other people might say about you.

Look back at Corey's example, and imagine what might have happened if Corey had had a weak inner Code.

With fear and insecurity in his heart, would Corey have given me the encouragement I needed? No. Even if he were a nice guy, something would have stopped him:

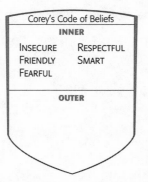

He might have resented my ability, or he might have been afraid that I would reject his idea.

Fortunately, Corey had courage and confidence in his heart, so he could give that same courage and confidence to me.

The proverb explains it well: "A good tree does not bear bad fruit, nor does a bad tree bear good fruit." If your heart is full of courage and confidence, you can give those gifts to others. But if your heart is full of fear and insecurity, then those will be your gifts.

That's why even when you're trying to help other people, it's still important to focus on your own heart first and to make sure your inner Code is strong.

The Friendship Balance

Giving others confidence will help you develop great friendships. But sometimes, you'll need to give confidence to yourself.

Back in college, my friend Beth had it all. She was brilliant, a sweet girl, knew tons of jokes, and was friends with everyone. I felt lucky to know her.

Since Beth was so cool, though, I often doubted whether she really wanted to be my friend. I kept thinking: "Man, this girl is too awesome to want to be friends with someone like me."

So I'd always ask Beth how she was doing, and we'd talk for hours. But for most of those hours, we'd talk about her. Only when we were about to hang up would Beth ask about me.

I realized that I had to do more than give kindness and encouragement to Beth. If I wanted a healthy friendship, I also had to give myself extra confidence — the confidence to share my life with her and to insist that she show an interest in me.

My experience with Beth taught me a valuable lesson. To have true friendships, you need to find the right balance:

❶ GIVE OTHERS CONSIDERATION. Put listening, encouragement, and other positive qualities at the center of your inner Code and give them to your friends.

AND

❷ GIVE YOURSELF CONFIDENCE. Share yourself with the other person and expect them to listen to you just as you're doing for them. If they don't do those things for you, give yourself the confidence either to ask them for more or to walk away from the friendship.

☛ YOUR TURN: No Thought of Reward

❶ Think about your two closest friends. How are you on the friendship balance? Think about how much consideration you give your friends and how much confidence you give yourself. If you're not in balance, what specific actions can you take to make the friendships better?

❷ There are a million ways you can contribute to your community. For example, I know a middle-school student who held a bake sale, raised $200, and gave the money to a refugee family. One high-school student built his cross-country team's unity by organizing a team dinner once a week. A girl I knew got friends to help her clean up a neighborhood park. What about you? What are two things you could do to contribute to your community?

❸ How about on an individual level: Can you give up your seat to someone on the bus, or join someone who's sitting by themselves at lunch? Write down at least one way you can give to a classmate, teacher, or anyone you run into during the day.

SEE IT THEIR WAY

One summer evening when I was fifteen, my sister Mehret and I sat in the living room, watching TV. We could hear the kitchen faucet in the background as my mother washed the dinner dishes. I had spent the day working, then playing basketball, and was now relaxing to *The Jeffersons*.

My father walked in and sat next to us, but we didn't notice him until he interrupted us: "I WOULD LIKE TO ASK YOU A QUESTION, IF I MAY. WHO AMONG YOU LOVES YOUR MOTHER?"

Mehret and I looked at each other, wondering what our crazy father was talking about now: *Is he seriously asking us if we love the woman who left friends and family for us, who carried us across a wilderness, who values our well-being above her own?*

"What are you talking about?" we said. "Of course we love her!"

70

Our father shook his head slowly:

"YOU ARE BOTH LIAR ONES. IF YOU TRULY LOVED YOUR MOTHER, SHE WOULDN'T BE COOKING FOR YOU ALL THE TIME AND SWEEPING FOR YOU ALL THE TIME AND WASHING FOR YOU ALL THE TIME. IF YOU LOVED HER, YOU WOULD LEAP WITH JOY TO DO THINGS FOR HER AND MAKE HER LIFE EASIER.

"BUT YOU LOVE YOURSELVES MUCH MORE THAN YOU LOVE YOUR MOTHER. YOU WOULD RATHER MAKE YOURSELVES HAPPY, WHICH IS WHY YOU SIT HERE WATCHING TV EVERY DAY WHILE SHE COOKS AND CLEANS FOR YOU. YOU DON'T KNOW WHAT LOVE IS."

I couldn't believe my father's nerve. What right did he have to tell me whom I loved and whom I didn't?

But the more I thought about his words, the more I realized their truth. How could I say I loved my mother when I didn't take one hour a week to make her life easier? When I had to be begged before I did anything around the house? When I expected a gold medal the few times I did something without being asked?

No, it was my mom who loved me. She gave to me

with no thought of reward. She sacrificed for me and loved me through her actions. Her love for me was a one-way street, with her doing all the loving, when it should have been a two-way boulevard, with me loving her back.

As furious as I was at my father, I had to admit that he had taught me a valuable lesson: *"I love you" isn't said through words, it's said through actions.*

Cheerleading Blues

The year after my father's tirade, Mehret ran into a big problem with him and my mom. She wanted to join the high-school cheerleading squad. For my parents, who had never even let her wear a short skirt, that was a joke. Their daughter, dressed in skimpy outfits? Prancing around in front of sex-crazed teenage boys? They'd throw her out of the house before they would let that happen.

Instead of getting upset or complaining, though, Mehret made a smart move: She put herself in my parents' shoes and asked the questions, *What do my parents want, and why?*

Once she put herself in their shoes, Mehret realized that my parents wanted her to be safe. So she asked the cheerleading team's faculty adviser to talk to my parents and to show them how the school kept the cheerleaders safe.

Mehret wanted to give my parents even more good reasons for letting her join the team, so she kept pushing her turbo button and asked herself: *What else can I do to make my parents see the value of cheerleading?*

She remembered that back when we were in elementary school, my parents used to awaken us at 5:00 A.M. to make us exercise. So she called my parents to the living room and showed them the stretches and jumps that cheerleading would teach her. Once my parents saw that Mehret would be safe and would get to exercise, they let her join. What can you learn from Mehret's story? The next time you face a challenge with your parents — or with anyone else — put yourself in the other person's shoes and try to see things their way. Like Mehret, you might be amazed by the results.

When Reason Fails

Obviously, there will be times when no matter how much you reason with your parents, things won't go your way, and you'll have to choose your reaction.

During my junior year of high school, my father and I got into a stupid argument, and neither one of us wanted to back down. Before long, we were barely speaking to each other, and my dad refused to let me attend my next track meet.

The next day, I felt awful when I had to tell my track coach I couldn't run. In fact, under different circumstances — if the next meet had been the state championship — I might have done something I never wanted to do: disobey my father. But in this instance, I realized that my relationship with my father mattered more than the next meet, so I swallowed my anger and came home early.

Giving to your parents — washing the car without being asked, coming home when you're supposed to, seeing things their way — will make them more likely to give you the things you want. More important, you'll build a better relationship with them.

Sometimes, though, conflicts will arise and no matter what you do, your parents will seem unreasonable. In these situations, remember that your parents are from another planet! Seriously, realize that your parents are people, too, and that no one is perfect. Just as you would want your parents to forgive you for your shortcomings, try to extend that same forgiveness to them.

No Matter Your Background

Unfortunately, some of us face agonizing family problems, where the issues are much greater than attending a track meet. Situations where our parents divorce, leaving us smack in the middle, unsure of what to do or feel. Or situations where our families abuse us, or where we don't have a family.

In these situations, when the simple answers don't apply, what do we do?

While there's no easy answer, I hope you'll consider these options:

❶ TALK TO SOMEONE YOU TRUST OUTSIDE YOUR FAMILY. This could be a teacher or spiritual adviser, your principal or a friend, or even a friend's parent. They might provide valuable guidance, so don't be afraid to ask. (If you need someone to talk to, I've put some helpful hotlines in the back of this book.)

❷ KEEP YOUR CODE STRONG. While you can't control who your parents are and what they do, you can always control who *you* are: You can always choose your own Code. Of course, maintaining an empowered Code amidst a rough family life is not easy. I hope the tools from "Win Every Day"— journaling and developing Spirit Builders — will help you overcome your challenges.

❸ ALWAYS KEEP HOPE ALIVE. As you'll see in the next Secret, even the most painful challenges can lift you to unimagined heights. So even if things are rough now, keep hope burning — keep believing that things will get better.

☛ **YOUR TURN:** SEE IT THEIR WAY

❶ Time to mind-read. Pick either a parent or a sibling and put yourself in their shoes. What kinds of things does that person think about? What are their biggest challenges? What kind of activities do they like to do?

Once you understand that person, you'll be able to give to them more effectively. For example, if you know that your sister is lonely, you might ask her to hang out with you and your friends. If you know your parents are overworked, you might help them around the house.

❷ Showing love isn't something we should do once in a while, it's something we should do all the time. So my challenge to you is this: Pick a time you're free every week — Sunday nights, Saturday mornings, or whatever works for you — and spend a few minutes planning how you'll show love to your friends and family in the coming week. You can even use your journal. Once you start this, showing love will become something you do regularly, not once in a while.

❸ If you're not on good terms with a family member, what's something you can do to improve the situation? Write down at least one thing you can do and something you can say that will improve the relationship. If it works, you might even make it part of your weekly routine!

GET IN THE GAME!

My little bro Hntsa is the man. My only complaint about him comes from when he was three years old. Whenever my father wanted to spank us older kids, he would send Hntsa to fetch the belt. Little Hntsa would come back with a big baseball bat instead!

Otherwise, Hntsa and I always got along growing up, except for a short time during his second year of high school.

Our little battle started because Hnsta didn't want to join any school activities. He would come home every day and either watch TV or play video games. Then he would do his homework.

My own high-school career had taught me that when you give to your school through activities, you always get back much more. So I couldn't stand to watch Hntsa miss out.

"Choose something, bro," I told him. "I don't care what you do, but you have to join a school activity."

"No," he insisted. "I don't want to. There's nothing I like."

"Too bad. Choose something."

"No. I'm not doing it. I'm not good at anything."

I almost gave in and let him have his way. But I cared too much about my brother. So I went to Mama, who I knew would take my side. I said, "Let me take all his video games to my apartment. Don't let him watch TV until he joins an activity."

Hnsta complained and complained until he realized that there was no way out. Then he joined the cross-country team.

He got slaughtered so badly that I thought he would quit. When I say "slaughtered," I mean back of the pack every race, out of hundreds of runners. Ouch!

Hnsta continued to struggle his junior year. But he kept trying. As hard as he tried, though, Hntsa never achieved the Hollywood ending: He never became one of his school's best runners.

But joining activities isn't about winning or losing. It's about whom you meet, what you learn, and whom you become while you're winning or losing. It's all about your journey, not your destination.

On his journey, Hntsa made more than twenty new friends. Friends who called him and asked him to hang out. Friends he didn't have before he joined the team.

Hntsa had also been chubby before he started running cross-country. By the time he graduated, he was in excellent shape. His self-confidence skyrocketed.

And guess who wrote Hnsta one of the letters of recommendation that helped him get into Duke University? His coach. The coach wrote, "In my twenty years of coaching, I can think of no athlete that I am more proud of."

You don't have to be the fastest or the top performer to get people's respect. You just have to try your best and not give up. I often have more respect for the kid who, despite losing, keeps trying 100 percent than I do for the kid who's winning. Why? Because it takes a heck of a lot more heart to keep going when you're down than when you're up.

One more thing happened to Hntsa during his journey — something even I never expected. Hntsa's team elected him as one of the captains for his senior year. Usually it's only the fast kids who get elected captain, and Hntsa wasn't even on varsity, let alone one of the top runners.

How did *he* become a captain? Just look at the top part of Hntsa's Code:

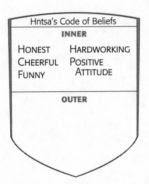

Even though Hntsa wasn't giving his team a first-place finish, he was providing something just as valuable: a great work ethic, humor, honesty, and a positive attitude.

He improved his teammates' morale and inspired the faster runners to do their best.

Let's add up what Hntsa would have missed out on if he hadn't gone out for the team: new friends, improved health, more self-confidence, a strong relationship with his coach, help with college admissions, leadership skills, and good times. Quite a lot, right? Hnsta thanks me now!

I want you to grow, too, so I'm going to give you the same advice I gave my little bro: Get in the Game! Even if you don't think you'll be good at an activity or don't know what activity you'll like, don't worry about it. Take a chance and get in there!

The Five Laws of Getting in the Game

Whether you're already involved in activities or are just getting started, The Five Laws of Getting in the Game will help you get the most out of your involvement.

Law #1: Start with what you like. Won't you work harder and perform better if you're doing something you enjoy? If you have no idea what activity you might like, you can ask your parents, counselor, or friends for advice. Remember, the activity can be outside of school — through a community center, religious group, or park district.

Law #2: Give invisible gifts. Don't just focus on what place you finish in or how many points you score. Give from the top half of your Code: Give hard work, enthusiasm, respect, and confidence. You'll be amazed at how much you get back.

Law #3: Give 110 percent effort to at least one activity. For the first three years of my high-school track career, I got spanked in practice and at meets. My senior year, I became the best on my team and ran in the state finals.

What fueled this transformation? I gave my running tremendous dedication: I ran thirty-five miles a week in the off-season, lifted weights, and recorded my progress on a chart in my journal.

Because I put everything I had into my sport, I performed at levels I never thought possible. You owe it to yourself to experience the amazing growth that comes from 110 percent effort — try it in at least one of your activities.

Law #4: Choose to make every activity fun. The

week before I started college, I signed up for a dorm crew that cleaned student bathrooms.

I was doing it for the cash, but during that week, I made much more than money. I met tons of new friends, including my second-year roommate, and had a blast getting to know the campus (and its smelly toilets!).

I got paid in so many ways other than money that I'd do it again for free. *Even cleaning bathrooms can be fun if you have the right attitude!*

Law #5: Try a variety of activities.

The summer after I graduated from Harvard, I tried something new: I flew to Colorado and helped high-school juniors write their college essays. While there, I heard the most inspiring speaker I'd ever encountered, a man named Derek Canty. After watching Derek for just a few hours, I realized I would love his job.

Trying something new showed me a whole new career. It might show you a new group of friends, a new skill, or knowledge about the world.

So don't just do the same old thing. Try new activities. Go to new places. Expand your horizons!

☛ **YOUR TURN:** GET IN THE GAME!

❶ When picking activities, always remember the first law of Getting in the Game: *Pick activities that you will enjoy.* If you choose things you like, you'll enjoy working hard and you'll have lots of fun.

For now, make a list of activities you enjoy. Of those, circle the one you'll definitely try to pursue this year.

❷ What happens if there's an activity you like, but your school or community doesn't offer it? For example, let's say you really like to dance, but your school doesn't have a dance program. Those who haven't pressed their turbo button might give up and look for something else. Those who've pressed their turbo button might ask the school if they can form a dance troop for the next assembly, or they might search online to see what other options are available in the community. Are there any activities that you would like to start at your school?

❸ Now, think about what you want to get out of your activities. Are you looking to meet people, to get in shape, or something else altogether? Just like setting specific goals helps you live out your Code, writing down what you want will help you get the most out of your time. For each activity, write down what you'd like to get out of it.

THE 4TH SECRET:

Never Lose Hope

You may win the Inner Battle and develop great relationships, but that alone is not enough: at some point, tremendous challenges will threaten to knock you off your feet — and they'll make living out your Code a much tougher task.

This Secret will help you survive those challenges and come out stronger.

To master this Secret, read and apply its crucial lesson:

- Never Give Up

NEVER GIVE UP

It was 4:00 A.M. in late December, and I was playing Nintendo Pro Wrestling during a church sleepover. Our group of seven high-school sophomores had spent the night devouring pizza and watching movies. We had no interest in sleeping.

Out of the corner of my eye, I saw our group leader, Mark. Why was he up? He had gone to bed hours earlier. Now he walked toward us with a grim look.

Mark pulled me aside from the group and shared the worst news I had ever received: My best friend, my hero, my brother Tewolde, had just been killed by a drunk driver.

It's not easy to share this story with you. Talking about my brother's passing opens up painful memories. But I'm sharing anyway, because I know that the way we help one another is by sharing real things about ourselves, not just surface-level gloss. I'm doing it because I know that no matter who you are, no matter how good you look or how much money you have, sooner or later, you're going to face challenges. Challenges that will rock you and change you, challenges that might uproot the most sacred beliefs in your Code.

After Tewolde died, I almost lost my will to keep going. My brother had survived refugee camps, wars, diseases — all the things that had killed millions back home. How could he be killed by something so avoidable? How could this caring, hardworking, beautiful person die, while the drunk driver walked away with only a broken toe?

My Code seemed meaningless. Why should I keep working hard and trying my best when this was the kind of garbage life would throw my way? Grades and scholarships seemed worthless compared to my brother's life.

I would have given up right then if I hadn't thought of some of my heroes. Of my mother, who left her friends and family and ventured into the wilderness, carrying me on her back for miles. My mother had faced far greater challenges than I had, yet she had never given up.

I also thought of another woman I had seen in the Ethiopian wilderness. Fleeing the war, she walked barefoot until the rocks and sand bloodied her feet, leaving a messy trail behind her. Despite unthinkable pain, she refused to give up. She kept limping and crawling.

Then I thought of Tewolde. That brother had never backed down from anything in his life. If he was looking down on me, nothing would disappoint him more than seeing me give up.

It was going to be the hardest thing I'd ever done, but I knew what I had to do. I had to honor all the courage I had seen and show some courage myself. It was my turn. So I told myself: *Mawi, this isn't going to be easy — it's going to be the hardest thing you've ever done. But you can do it.*

Instead of giving up on your life dreams, dream twice as much. Learn twice as much, run twice as fast, show twice as much love for others — do it for yourself and for your brother.

That's the choice I made after my brother passed away. That choice has been the difference between success and despair.

I hope you never have to deal with anything so terrible. I wouldn't wish that on anyone. But I guarantee you one thing: You *will* face adversity at some point. When that adversity comes, I hope you'll think of the heroes in your life — and of all the people around the world who face challenges every day — and remember that we all have it within us to show our own kind of bravery.

Getting Lost

After the anquish of losing my brother, I never imagined that anything could hurt worse. But during my second year of college, I dealt with an even greater devastation: the complete collapse of my inner Code.

My first year at Harvard was great: I made friends, earned outstanding grades, and did my best to live out my Code. I was pretty sure that I had things under control.

Then came the second year and a barrage of unexpected challenges. The very first day, my computer's hard drive self-destructed. In one of my classes, I had a run-in with the teacher and got an F on a major paper. In sports,

I hurt my knee and had to take a break from running long-distance.

But that was just the beginning. It seemed that everywhere I turned that year, something new chipped away at my inner Code.

In my classes, many of the books I read for my history major tore at my most basic values. Their authors argued that history was determined by big forces like countries, and that the human beings who made up those countries — people like you and me — were little more than pawns.

That set me back. I began to doubt whether I could make the world a better place. I began to doubt the power of the turbo button. I began to doubt the importance of hard work, love, respect, and all the things I had put in the top half of my Code.

Looking for relief, I started talking to my classmates. But unlike in Wheaton, where almost everyone thought the way I did, my Harvard classmates often had a different worldview. I talked with Buddhists, Muslims, Jews, Christians, and atheists; billionaires, millionaires, and folks on Welfare like me; people from every ethnicity under the sun.

The more talking I did, the more I realized that my classmates, many of whom I admired and respected, had different Codes than I did. Not just different outer goals, but core values that were different — sometimes in complete opposition to my own. I began to wonder whether my Code was a good one — and to doubt more and more the beliefs I lived my life by.

Then came that summer — the hardest summer of my entire life. As the boss at a camp for elementary-school students, I had six counselors who worked for me.

Every day, I lived by my Code; every day, I tried to be honest, hardworking, and as kind as I could be. But still, three of the six counselors couldn't stand me! They weren't just unfriendly, they did everything they could to mess up the camp. They talked behind my back, disobeyed the rules — one counselor even took her first-graders to a bar!

By summer's end, I saw no way I could believe in things like respect and hard work — they certainly hadn't helped me all year.

One day, I woke up with a piercing realization: I had lost my Code. I no longer knew what values I should live by.

93

If you've never been through an overwhelming challenge, you might not understand how I felt. When I tell you that losing my Code was tougher than losing my brother, I'm not exaggerating.

Losing my Code was like trying to play the most important basketball game of my life, the game that would determine my happiness forever. But instead of a basketball, I found myself holding a cucumber. Instead of referees, ostriches paced the sidelines. Instead of baskets, I had to shoot at huge piles of toilet paper.

No matter how hard I tried, I couldn't win because I didn't know what the game was anymore. I couldn't even keep score.

That's what I felt like by the end of my sophomore year. I had always thought that I understood the game of life, but suddenly I didn't have a clue. I still missed my brother, but I no longer believed that the principles he had lived by mattered. I still wanted to be a good person, but I didn't understand why or how.

As I looked for friends to talk to about my challenges, I realized that I knew almost everybody but didn't *really* know anybody. I knew people on the surface, but there were few I felt comfortable opening up to.

By the end of that summer, I was filling my journal with some depressing thoughts:

> *I feel myself dropping to an all-time low tonight, almost as low as the time the bro left ... perhaps this is just a continuation of that long night ... perhaps it has always been nighttime for me.*

> *I feel like life has no meaning. What's the point anyway? I find no beauty anywhere.*

I was stuck in a pit, and I couldn't even see a way out. If someone had told me what I had to do to feel better, I would have done it in a second. But I had no idea how to help myself.

So what did I do? When nothing I did worked, when my sense of purpose was lost, when depression clouded my world, I did the only thing I could. I dug through the rubble of my Code and picked the fundamental ideals that I could still try to uphold — ideals like treating people with respect and loving my family.

Even though I was lost, my heart told me that these ideals were still right and that I should still center my Code around them. I also tried to relieve my mind by throwing myself into activities. I did community service, played intramural sports whenever my knee allowed, and even studied abroad in Spain for a semester. It wasn't easy, but like the woman in the sand, I kept crawling that year and the next year, hoping that I would someday reach greener pastures.

It took a lot of time, a lot of thought, and a lot of effort, but eventually, I reconstructed my Code. I decided that I still wanted to base my life around things like hard work, respect for others, and the power of taking action to improve your life.

Why am I sharing this horrific story with you?

I want you to realize that when the most central and deep-rooted beliefs in your Code get challenged, you may feel like the ground is slipping out from under you.

If you ever fall into depression, I hope you'll have

close friends to talk to, adults you can share your problems with, and the courage and confidence to seek counseling. Looking back, I wish I had asked for more help. I didn't realize that it's hard to pull yourself out of depression and that there were people I could have turned to for support — like the people I've listed in the hotlines at the back of this book.

There's one other reason why I'm sharing this story: I want you to know that I wasn't always on a track to success and I wasn't always a star at Harvard. I've known heartache, and I've been tempted many times to give up.

Many people who succeed experience tremendous challenges. Their success may seem to come easily, but they struggle just like you and me. The reason they succeed is that they refuse to give up.

So if you're struggling in school or being harassed by classmates or facing a million other challenges that could arise, don't ever think that your challenges will prevent you from succeeding. You *can* succeed. In fact, as you'll soon learn, your challenges can often be your best friends.

SECRET CODE CONNECT: Never Lose Hope

When challenges strike and nothing goes your way, your inner Code can crumble just like mine did. At times like that, you'll need to rely on the foundations you've built: your friends, your Spirit Builders, and the goals you've been working toward every day.

Since you can't predict when challenges will hit you, start working on those foundations today, so they'll be there when you need them.

Consider the two Codes below: Which of these two people do you think is more likely to overcome challenges?

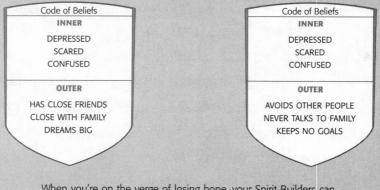

Code of Beliefs	Code of Beliefs
INNER	**INNER**
DEPRESSED	DEPRESSED
SCARED	SCARED
CONFUSED	CONFUSED
OUTER	**OUTER**
HAS CLOSE FRIENDS	AVOIDS OTHER PEOPLE
CLOSE WITH FAMILY	NEVER TALKS TO FAMILY
DREAMS BIG	KEEPS NO GOALS

When you're on the verge of losing hope, your Spirit Builders can inspire you and remind you why you're special. You goals can give you a reason to keep dreaming. If you don't have either, though, your challenges might drown you.

Your Worst Enemy and Your Best Friend

I read a quote recently that made my blood boil:

> *"We succeed in life not despite our challenges but because of our challenges."*

I couldn't believe that anyone would say that. How could losing my brother or enduring depression help me succeed? I wish I had my brother back. I wish I had enjoyed my sophomore year of college.

The more I thought about the quote, though, the more I realized its wisdom.

Do you know what gave me the extra motivation to study harder, run harder, and show more courage in high school? It was my brother's passing. After my brother passed away, I decided, Hey, I've got to make something of my life. If I don't help my family, who will?

Do you know why I'm writing this book? Why I speak around the country? Why I think so much about success and happiness? It's because I was once depressed, because I lived in that pit for a full year. That pit was so nasty that I told myself, *Once I figure out how to get out of here, I'm gonna help other people get out too.* And now I get so much happiness from helping others.

Of course, when I was going through the challenges, I didn't see that anything good could come of them. But now I realize that both my brother's death and my bout with depression forced me to grow in unimagined ways and to come back with an even stronger Code than I had in the past.

So should we wish for challenges? Of course not! Give me my brother back and I'll trade you Harvard and every other accomplishment I've had.

But since we can't control many of the challenges that hit us, shouldn't we at least use them to take ourselves higher? Shouldn't we get something good out of all the pain and suffering?

One thing is for sure: It's not whether you will encounter challenges or even whether your challenges will change you. The challenges will come, and they will change you.

The only real question is *how* your challenges will change you. For better or for worse? That is your choice.

☞ YOUR TURN: NEVER GIVE UP

❶ Often, when challenges strike, people focus only on the negative and forget about all the positive things in their life. For instance, during my sophomore year at Harvard, I didn't consider that I had excelled in school, or that for several years, I had lived out an awesome Code. What are some positives in your life? How will you remind yourself of those positives when challenges strike you?

❷ Pick a challenge from your past and decide how you can get inspiration from it. For example, my brother died in December, so I've declared December to be Honorary Tewolde Month. Throughout the month, I look for ways to celebrate his spirit.

Maybe you've lost a loved one, or a pet, or don't see one of your parents often. Whatever challenge you've faced, how can you use it to lift yourself higher?

❸ Sometimes we view minor challenges — little obstacles to our outer goals, like a bad grade, getting cut from a school play, or getting turned down for a date — as if they're unbearable, life-altering setbacks. Think over the past few months: What are some molehills that you've turned into mountains? How will you react the next time a challenge like that hits you?

❹ If you had a major challenge today, who are the friends, relatives, or advisers you would go to for help? If you don't have any close friends, write down the names of a few friends whom you want to get to know better. If you like, you can include family members and advisers, such as teachers or counselors.

❺ Do you have any friends who are going through challenges right now? Write their names and some ways that you can help them get through their hard times.

#

Take Smart Risks

THERE'S A FINAL FACTOR THAT HAS OVERWHELMING POWER: RISK TAKING. IT CAN LAUNCH YOU TO NEW HEIGHTS OR DROP YOU TO UNIMAGINED LOWS, ALL IN A SINGLE MOMENT.

TO MAKE YOUR DREAMS COME TRUE, YOU'LL NEED COURAGE. TO AVOID FLUSHING YOUR DREAMS DOWN THE TOILET, YOU'LL NEED WISDOM. THIS SECRET'S TWO SECTIONS WILL HELP YOU DEVELOP THESE STRENGTHS.

- TAKE LEAPS OF FAITH
- RESPECT THE MOMENT

TAKE LEAPS OF FAITH

N o way! There was no way I was going to Harvard. That's what I decided as soon as I got my acceptance letters from colleges.

I told my parents, friends, and guidance counselor that I had chosen Washington University in Saint Louis over Harvard. I thought I would be more comfortable at Washington. I wanted to be closer to home. And although I didn't mention it to my parents, at Wash U. I had met two beautiful young ladies!

Deep inside, though, I knew my real reason for choosing Washington: Harvard scared the heck out of me. Wheaton North High School was one thing. You could do well at Wheaton North by working hard and respecting others.

But Harvard? Harvard was where the real-deal smart

people, the geniuses, the Einsteins went. There was no way that a ghetto, Welfare, refugee brother like Mawi could hang on that level just by working hard.

What if everyone was rich and snobby? What if I looked stupid? What if I flunked out?

When you get into Harvard, they mail you a postcard asking whether you will attend. If you don't return it by May 1, your spot goes to someone on the waiting list. Most kids send back the postcard the minute they get it. Not me. Just one week before the deadline, I still hadn't mailed mine. Time was running out. Then, study hall on April 25, 1995, changed my life.

After finishing my assignments, I found myself with nothing to do, so I reached into my backpack and pulled out a stack of note cards. I was following my brother Tewolde's example; he used to write his favorite quotes on note cards and look at them whenever he had time.

One of the quotes stopped me in my tracks. It challenged me to push myself higher than I'd ever thought possible. Here's what the quote said:

"If you want miracles to happen in your life, you have to have some faith."

I realized that if I wanted to experience amazing things, I had to take some risks. I had to venture into territory that made me feel uncomfortable.

Even though Harvard scared me, I knew that deep inside, I wanted the challenge. I had worked for years to develop my mind, and for as long as I had kept a journal, I had been telling myself that I was as smart as anyone. If that belief was part of my inner Code, why should I stop believing it now?

I rose from my seat and walked out of study hall — I didn't even stop for a pass. I marched straight to my great friend, my counselor Mrs. Martin. She wasn't at her desk, but I left her a note — a note she kept for a long time afterward. It read: *I decided during study hall today, I'm gonna go to Harvard.*

You saw in the last chapter that I went through some rough, rough times at Harvard. *Just because you have*

THE 5TH SECRET: **TAKE SMART RISKS**

enough courage to take the risky path doesn't mean that the risky path will be easy.

But I also experienced miracles at Harvard. I thought I wouldn't fit in, I thought I wouldn't do well in classes. But I excelled in both areas. After my four years were up, my classmates elected me a Class Marshal, one of their life-time representatives. More important than any positions or grades, though, I expanded my mind by leaps and bounds, and I made friends that I'll keep as long as I live.

What kind of life do you want for yourself? Do you want a dull one, where you don't pursue your dreams? Or do you want an adventure, full of courage, hope, and miracles? The choice is yours.

Everyone Fails

Many people take the dull path because they fear failure. But successful people succeed only because they have the courage to take leaps of faith.

Even the greatest basketball player ever, Michael

Jordan, is no stranger to failure. He was asked about it once; here's what Mike had to say:

"I have missed more than 9,000 shots in my career. I have lost almost 300 games. On 26 occasions I have been entrusted to take the game-winning shot . . . and missed. And I have failed over and over and over again in my life. And that is why . . . I succeed."

Failure goes hand in hand with success. Any time you try to succeed, you risk failure. *But if you never try, you'll fail every single time.*

To go on that dream date, you have to ask the other person out; to make the game-winning shot, you have to risk that you might miss it; to attend the college you want, you have to apply there in the first place.

If you don't try, you'll end up no better off than if you had failed: You'll have no date, no glorious game-winning shot, and no dream education. In fact, you'll be worse off — you won't even have the satisfaction of knowing that at least you tried.

Destiny's Child

The music group Destiny's Child has sold millions of albums, and their lead singer, Beyoncé Knowles, starred in the third *Austin Powers* movie.

For a while, though, it looked like the women of Destiny's Child were destined to fail.

When they were first getting started, they took a leap of faith and tried out for a TV talent competition called *Star Search.* Even though they had skills and had worked hard, they got cut in the final round. They were so disappointed, they went to the show's host to find out what he thought.

You know what he told them? *It's the groups that don't win right away that usually end up making it big.*

As the *Star Search* host explained, the folks who win right away often get comfortable and think that they've made it. But those folks who try and at first don't succeed? They're forced to ask: *How can I improve?* They push themselves to work even harder, and eventually, they make themselves much better than they ever were in the first place.

As painful as failure is, it can also help you in the long run. So when you try and don't reach your goal, don't think that you've failed. Instead, push yourself to learn from the experience, and vow to do better the next time.

True Success

Some of you might look at my story and think, "Mawi, you were probably successful all your life. What do you know about failure?"

What I know is that I've failed more times than I can count. I failed when I couldn't make the Freshman "A" basketball team; when I stayed home on my prom night; when I got a D in eighth-grade math class. I've failed all my life, and I still fail today.

The reason I've had some outer success is that I don't

let my failures keep me down. I get up and try again, hopefully a little smarter.

Along my journey, I've learned the truth about success: Success doesn't mean reaching all your goals, it means leading yourself, Winning your Inner Battle, and having the courage to pursue your dreams.

SECRET CODE CONNECT: Take Leaps of Faith

There's a reason why they call a leap of faith a "leap of faith." It requires faith in yourself and the courage to take the leap.

Of the two people whose Codes you see below, which is more likely to take daring leaps of faith?

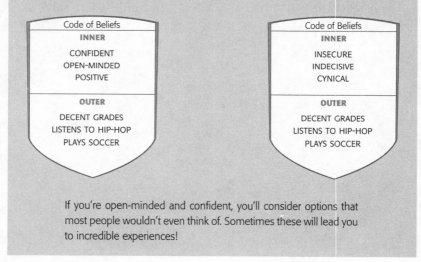

Code of Beliefs		Code of Beliefs
INNER		**INNER**
CONFIDENT		INSECURE
OPEN-MINDED		INDECISIVE
POSITIVE		CYNICAL
OUTER		**OUTER**
DECENT GRADES		DECENT GRADES
LISTENS TO HIP-HOP		LISTENS TO HIP-HOP
PLAYS SOCCER		PLAYS SOCCER

If you're open-minded and confident, you'll consider options that most people wouldn't even think of. Sometimes these will lead you to incredible experiences!

☞ YOUR TURN: TAKE LEAPS OF FAITH

❶ Everyone has something that they've wanted to do but haven't tried because they were afraid. It might be trying out for a sports team or a school play, studying a new language, or asking out someone you've always had a crush on. What risk have you been holding out on?

❷ Okay, so you've admitted what leap of faith scared you — that took courage. Now, how would it feel if you took that risk and it worked out? Write down the feeling.

❸ How do you want to respond the next time you fail to reach one of your goals? Write about how you might react differently than you have in the past.

❹ Want to really press your turbo button? Combine the 3rd Secret ("Give First, Receive Second") and the 5th Secret ("Take Smart Risks"), and act as a Spirit Builder in encouraging your friends to pursue their dreams. You could be the extra push they need to leap toward their dream! To do this, write down the name of someone you know and what leap of faith they're holding back on. Then write what you can do to help them take the plunge.

RESPECT THE MOMENT

I went to Germany last year with five college friends to visit my old roommate Justin. While walking in a park in Munich, we stopped to rest in front of a stream. Somehow, we fell to talking about who could jump the stream, and my friends dared me to try it. They promised me ten euros each — about fifty dollars total.

I looked the stream over. It was about fourteen feet wide, with jagged rocks cropping up here and there near its shores. If I fell short and landed on the rocks, I would be a bloody mess. "I could jump it, no problem," I told them. "But I don't feel like it."

That got them going: "We have a new name for Mawi — Jumps-the-Least Asgedom."

As we kept walking, we noticed something interesting: Halfway across the stream, two feet above the water, lay a catwalk — a narrow ledge on which I could land. It ran along the middle of the stream as far as the eye could see.

They started daring me again. "Surely, you can jump to the middle. You don't have to jump all the way now. Come on! Do it."

My Code would have told me it was stupid, that I could still hurt myself, that fifty dollars was nothing compared to my health. But I got caught up in the moment. I knew I could make the jump, and I wanted to shut my friends up, so I decided to try it.

After stepping back to get a little start, I sprang forward and jumped the seven feet. My feet touched the catwalk, and I tried to stop. But I had too much forward momentum. I kept going and landed in the stream.

I hadn't realized how fast the stream was moving until I was in it. In no time at all, it swept me away. I was in trouble, but I hadn't panicked. Yet.

I reached my left hand up to the catwalk wall — about two feet high — and started pulling myself up. But the current was too strong. I felt a sudden jerk and my left shoulder popped out of its socket. Pain exploded through my arm, and I fell back into the water.

Now I was in serious trouble. The current had taken me farther downstream, and I didn't know what lay ahead — rocks, rapids, or maybe even a waterfall.

One bad decision, and I had put my life in danger. One moment of trying to prove I was cool, and twenty-five years of hard work and perseverance were on the line.

Who knows what would have happened if it hadn't been for my friend Justin. Realizing my predicament, he leaped onto the catwalk, landed perfectly, and sprinted until he caught up with me. Despite the intense pain, I lifted my left arm and he pulled me up.

Five months later, my shoulder still hurts. Each time I feel the pain, I remember that one poor decision almost destroyed my entire Code.

One Moment Can Become Forever

One moment, my family was stuck in a refugee camp; the next moment, we were on our way to America. One moment, my brother was alive; the next moment, he was dead.

Our lives can change in one moment. Sometimes we control the moments; sometimes we don't. Sometimes we want the moments to come; other times we don't.

But all it takes for our lives to change is that one moment.

As a teenager, I didn't always realize this. My brother and I once stole a parking meter and tried to take the money. We did it because we were poor. We did it because it seemed fun. We did it because we were bored.

The cops missed us by moments. They chased us and almost had us.

If we had gotten caught, that moment would have changed our lives. I probably would have gone to a juvenile-detention center — if my dad had let me live that long. I might never have attended Harvard. I might not be writing this book.

But when we were stealing the meter, we never thought about the consequences. We never stopped to think, *What if . . . ?*

The last thing I want to do is preach, but I'd be cheating you if I didn't warn you: Your life can change in one moment. One dumb decision, like driving drunk or resorting to violence, can make your Code much harder to live. You might still reach your goals, but it will be much more difficult, and you'll have put yourself through a whole bunch of unnecessary pain.

The Code Breakers

Unfortunately, it's not just *your* actions that can get you in trouble. You also have to think about what your friends are doing.

When I was 13, I had a friend named Fred. Every time I hung out with Fred, I *almost* got arrested.

One time we climbed the roof of his four-story apartment building and discovered thousands of pebbles. Fred started tossing pebbles at the cars below us, and I joined in — not trying to hurt anyone, just trying to have a little fun. But the neighbors didn't find it funny — they knew that those pebbles could crack someone's wind-

SECRET CODE CONNECT: Respect the Moment

When I was 16, a drunk driver killed my brother. When I was 21, another drunk driver killed my father. Neither of the drunk drivers wanted to kill anyone, but they killed two innocent people. How did it happen?

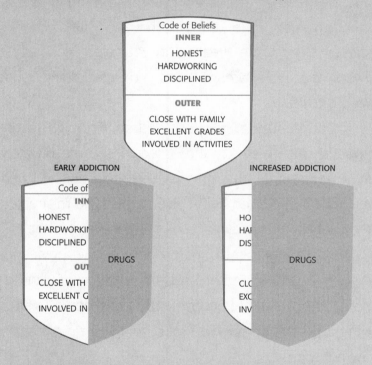

Both drivers were under the influence of alcohol. Alcohol and other drugs have an effect on our minds — the more powerful the drug, the more dangerous the effect. Once you take a drug, you're agreeing not to be in your right mind. You're agreeing to give up control of your Code.

shield and cause an accident. They called the police, and we barely escaped.

Time after time, Fred was getting me into trouble like that. Fred is what I call a Code Breaker: a friend who is bound to destroy the goals you have in your Code. Do you have any Code Breakers in your life? Friends that always lead you wrong? If so, consider doing what Deadra did.

I met Deadra at a special school for high-school dropouts. After I spoke, she asked to see me privately and told me about her boyfriend. He told her he loved her, and she believed him — even though he mistreated her, got high every day, and sometimes even hit her.

We examined her life: Before she met her boyfriend, she was in school and had a great relationship with her mom. Once she met her boyfriend — and then moved in with him — she dropped out of school and almost never saw her mom.

To an outsider, Deadra's choice would seem obvious: leaving her boyfriend would be the right thing to do. But Deadra really cared about him, and she didn't want to abandon him. I figured she would probably stay with him, no matter how poorly he treated her.

Well, a few months later, I heard from Deadra again. As hard as it was, she recognized that unless she left her boyfriend, she would never have control of her life. Deadra made a life-changing decision: She left him, moved back to her mom's, got back in school, and made a vow that her next boyfriend would bring her up, not down.

☛ YOUR TURN: RESPECT THE MOMENT

❶ In the 1st Secret, you created your Code and thought about your goals. On a separate sheet or in your journal, list three things you won't do because they might prevent you from reaching your goals.

❷ It could happen that someone — your friend, your brother or sister, or someone else — will pressure you to try one of the three things you just wrote about above. To give yourself motivation to stay strong, write down what the consequences of each action would be.

❸ Are there any Code Breakers in your life? What steps can you take to surround yourself with friends who will help you live your Code, rather than destroy it?

CONCLUSION

WE'RE ALMOST DONE, AND I HOPE YOU'VE ENJOYED THE JOURNEY. BEFORE YOU MOVE ON, PLEASE CONSIDER MY FINAL ADVICE ON NAVIGATING THE REAL WORLD.

IN THE CONCLUSION, YOU'LL FIND THE FOLLOWING PARTING LESSONS:

- REAL SUCCESS
- THE CODE

REAL SUCCESS

MTV has a show called *The Real World*, where a group of folks my age hang out, party, have fun jobs, and live together for free in a PHAT pad. I like the show, but I've noticed something about it: it's not about the real world.

If you want to understand the "real" real world, consider my father's story.

When he lived in Ethiopia, his village lacked doctors. So my father delivered babies, treated snakebite, and healed malaria victims. Working in the countryside, he brought life to thousands.

Then he came to America and worked the only job he could find: scrubbing toilets. In the Ethiopian countryside, no one had cared that my father didn't have his high-school diploma. But here in America, it's a different story. In this country, it's almost impossible to work any good job — much less be a doctor — if you haven't educated yourself.

That's the "real" real world: Educate yourself, or else. If MTV wanted to show the "real" real world, they'd pick two people: one who worked hard as a kid, got educated, and had money to pay rent or buy a PHAT pad; the other who ignored school and ended up scrubbing toilets.

Not that you have to take the traditional college route. I have a friend who loves to work on cars; he dreams of owning a car-repair shop. He's enrolled in auto-tech school, and next year, he's taking business classes. He's living out his Code and looking out for his future.

Another teen I know wants to be a chef, so she's working at a restaurant, saving up for culinary school, and practicing her cooking on the side.

Still another friend, who struggled with standardized tests and got average grades in college, has charm and a mind for business. He found his calling as a financial adviser, and now he makes $100,000 a year at a job he loves. But if he had dropped out of school, his current employer wouldn't have hired him, no matter how strong his Code.

What's the point of all these stories? We live in a

society that values education. Whether it's fair or not, if you haven't educated yourself, many people will respect you less, pay you less, and value you less. So don't trap yourself into making high school pay the rest of your life.

If you've dropped out of high school or haven't done well, that doesn't have to stop you. You can still create a bright future for yourself. But you have to educate yourself and start now.

The Karate Kid

You may wonder what specific things you can do to get into college. Before I tell you, I'd like to share a story from the movie *The Karate Kid.*

In the movie, a teenager named Daniel visits old Mr. Miyagi's house to learn karate. But Miyagi doesn't teach Daniel karate kicks and punches; instead, he makes Daniel wax the car, paint the fence, and sand the floor. After weeks of frustration, Daniel storms out.

Just then, Miyagi asks to see how Daniel waxed the

car. Daniel leans over and demonstrates the circular waxing motion that Miyagi showed him earlier. When Miyagi suddenly swings at him, Daniel blocks Miyagi's punch! It turns out that the waxing motion was the same motion a karate champion would use to block a punch.

The same thing happens with the other chores. While Daniel was painting and sanding, he was also learning how to block kicks and low punches.

If you think about it, you're a lot like Daniel. While reading the stories in this book, you've gotten more than just entertainment. You've learned how to take control of your mind, and as a bonus, you now know almost everything you need to get into college!

Want to see what I mean? Let's examine what they ask for on the typical college application:

Activities: Most college applications will ask you to list your involvement in activities. Why? Because colleges don't want students who will just sit in their dorm rooms all day; they want students who will make their campuses vibrant. They want students who learn inside *and* outside the classroom.

Some students have just been sitting on their behinds through high school. Not you. You read and applied "Get in the Game!" and through your activities, you expanded your horizons, achieved things you never knew you could, and made new friends. And on top of all that, you've built your college résumé!

Recommendations: Many colleges will ask you for letters of recommendation from your counselor and teachers. Why? Because colleges don't just want smart folks, they want smart folks who care about people. Would you want 5,000 smart jerks at your school?

Some students couldn't get a recommendation from their friends, let alone their teachers. But you read and applied "Give First, Receive Second" and showed love to everyone in your community without expecting a thing in return. Now you have close bonds with your friends, family, teachers, and counselors. And guess what: Some of those folks will hook you up with sweet recommendations! Proceed, young warrior!

Grades: All colleges will ask to see your grades. Some students never believed that they could do well, so they didn't bother to try. But not you.

You learned in "Win the Inner Battle" that you can earn good grades by controlling your beliefs and working hard. So you applied yourself in school, learned a wealth of information, developed a work ethic that'll last you a lifetime, and earned the best grades possible. Grade barrier? Destroyed!

Essays and test scores: The last pieces of getting into college, your test scores and your personal essay, might be scarier. But if you've been working hard in school and learning as much as you can, you should do fine on the tests. And if you've been taking smart risks and showing courage, you'll not only have made your life more exciting, but you'll also have plenty of captivating stories to tell in your essay.

So you're set. You already know most of what you need to know to be competitive in college admissions. You have just one story left.

Nothing Outside You

When she got the letter, Susan Marshall-Bleser was totally dejected. She had done everything she was supposed to in high school — she earned excellent grades, showed her teachers respect, and got involved with more than a dozen school activities. Still, her dream college — Duke University — had sent her a rejection letter. Susan learned the hard way how competitive college admissions can be.

The next fall, when she went to her second-choice school — Miami University in Ohio — Susan decided to make the most out of her college experience. Instead of dwelling on what might have been at Duke, she did her best at Miami: She worked hard in classes, gave encouragement and goodwill to everyone she met, and con- tributed to her community and her activities.

After graduating from Miami, Susan found that her hard work paid off: a major advertising agency was im- pressed with Susan's grades and hired her, even though Susan had no advertising experience.

Respecting her teachers paid off, too. When she wanted to get better at writing commercials, Susan got help from an unlikely source: her high-school theater teacher. That teacher's husband helped Susan, even though Susan hadn't taken the teacher's class in over five years.

Being kind to others and getting involved also paid off. Susan now has more friends than anyone else I know — hundreds of friends, all over the country!

Susan didn't get into her ideal college, but she's achieved outer success on so many levels: as an ad writer, as a radio announcer, as an actress in Chicago, and most important, with her family and friends.

What can we learn from her story?

While certain colleges might open extra doors for

you, in the end, the true question won't be what college you attended, but <u>what you did at the college you attended.</u> Did you learn a lot? Did you have fun? Did you make good friends? These are the questions to ask yourself, not just during college, but during middle school, high school, and the rest of your life.

So as you think about your future, don't put too much pressure on yourself. Try your best to get into the college of your choice, but always remember that the Code you put in your heart is much more powerful than the diploma you'll hang on your wall.

☞ YOUR TURN: REAL SUCCESS

❶ Earlier in your Code, you wrote about your beliefs and some goals you'd like to accomplish. Take this opportunity to look back at your outer goals. Then return to this page and write down the most important one.

❷ To accomplish those goals, what type of education will you need? For instance, to be a doctor, you have to graduate from college and medical school; to be a teacher, you need a college degree and perhaps a graduate degree; and many skilled positions, such as mechanics and machinists, require a high-school diploma or business training. Write down the education you'll need. If you don't know the answer, you can find out by getting online or asking a teacher or school counselor.

❸ Remember: While you want to aim for a destination, the journey is what's important about life. For example, many people make their best friendships in college, and while doctors are attending medical school, they learn important lessons about science that will help them in everyday life. What would you like to gain from your educational journey?

THE CODE

A friend who's an amateur pilot once shared with me the most confusing part of flying. He said that sometimes while he's cruising through the air, he looks down toward the ground, and he's sure his plane is going the wrong way. The instruments in front of him tell him he's on the right path, but his eyes tell him otherwise.

Once, while flying over Colorado, he was so sure the instruments were wrong that he abandoned them and started to follow his eyes. But the instruments weren't wrong — he got lost and had to make his way back hundreds of miles.

Now he knows: Trust the instruments, even when your eyes are telling you something else.

In this book, I've shared with you five instruments — The 5 Secrets — that will guide you to success. But they will help you only if you have faith and follow them, even when your eyes tell you to do otherwise.

Sometimes you'll look around your school, and you'll see that folks who Take First and Give Later are getting ahead. Other times, you'll encounter folks who take stupid risks and are extraordinarily popular. Your eyes will tell you that to succeed or to be popular, you should Take First and Give Later, or take stupid risks.

When this happens, remember my friend the pilot; don't let your eyes mislead you.

In my own teen experience, I struggled for years to build my confidence; I had to spend semester after semester working hard in classes; and I gave respect to hundreds of folks before I got outer rewards, such as college scholarships. Sometimes I couldn't see any outer rewards — and I wondered if they would ever come. But they did come, and in much bigger ways than I ever could have imagined.

So as you fly toward your dreams, keep your eyes on The 5 Secrets: Win the Inner Battle; Win Every Day; Give

135

First, Receive Second; Never Lose Hope; and Take Smart Risks. They won't always bring you glamour or instant results. But if you keep your eyes on them, The 5 Secrets will guide you to lasting success.

Much Respect

Many people talk about improving their lives but won't do anything to learn how. By taking the time to read *The Code,* you've proven yourself different — and I have much respect for you.

Now, you're ready for the true challenge: applying what you've learned. If all you do is read *The Code,* and you don't apply its Secrets, it won't do you much good. *The Code* will help you only if you make it a part of your life. So I challenge you.

I challenge you to create a new Code for yourself as soon as you finish this book and to post that Code in your room.

I challenge you to remember: Success doesn't come

*from winning once or once in a while — it comes from Winning the Inner Battle **every day.***

Some days, you will try your best and not reach your goals. I challenge you to never lose hope. Remember what the great philosopher Lao Tzu said: "Failure is the foundation of success, and the means by which it is achieved."

If you ever need inspiration or a refresher on The 5 Secrets, I'll be waiting for you here in these pages. Come by any time!

Make Your Life Special

The 5 Secrets didn't just appear to me in a dream. I discovered The 5 Secrets because I had family and friends who supported me, and because I had an amazing brother who taught me how to give before he passed away.

Now that I've shared The 5 Secrets with you, I hope you won't just use the knowledge to focus on your own success.

I hope you'll help others succeed, too: that you'll stick up for the folks who need help and lend courage to those who need it; that you'll leave our world a little kinder and more beautiful than you found it.

If you do — if you do walk with courage and confidence, if you give more than you take, if you keep your Code before you — I know that you will make your life special.

Thanks for letting me share my life and ideas with you, and until next time — *May The Code be with you!*

Your Friend,

ACKNOWLEDGMENTS

This book would not be possible without the following Spirit Builders:

To the best rappers in America, the students at Canter Middle School in Chicago, for helping me create the sample Codes for the book and sharing their raps with me.

To some of the brightest middle-school students I've ever met, Mrs. Gunnell's seventh-grade class, for your fantastic comments editing this book.

To the following friends who reviewed drafts of this book: Julie Thompson, Jeff Sears, Tori, Sarah Gudmundson, Sheila Conley, Andy and Doug Rowland, Christian Champ, Bobbi Wheatley, Brett and Emily Stousland, Emanuel Brown, T.S., Selam Daniel, Yvonne Weinstein, Raimonda Mikatavage, Chris Liccardi, PJ Karafiol; DeEtte Sauer; Sue Ferrara, and Michelle Peterson.

Special thanks to Annette Hartman and Chad Wathington for reading multiple drafts and to Christy Waldhoff for sharing so many fantastic ideas.

To my boy, Bill Triant, for your amazing insights and continual support — thank you, too, for being worse than me at basketball, so that I always have someone to beat ☺!

To an outstanding marketing firm, Monograph Communication Group, for helping me with my Web site, and all aspects of my business — thanks, Kyle, Brett, and Mike.

To my friends Mark Linsz and Todd Decker — for your enthusiasm and continual support.

To my new friend, Mike Boraz, and Michelle too, for your warmth, kindness, and helping me edit this book.

To the wonderful folks in my old school district, Illinois District 200, for your tremendous support and enthusiasm.

To my friends, Lynn Dieter, Teri Voss, Ben Kaplan, Josh and Kim Lang, and Becky Liscum, for all your love and support.

To the wonderful folks in Highland Park, Illinois, at School District 112, Guy Schumacher and company, much thanks and respect.

To Tara Burkhart, Nan Cosier, and Lincoln Hall middle school; and to Lisa Hoffman's class at Gower Middle School for helping edit this book.

To Karen Wadsworth and Tracey Daniels at Media Masters Publicity, thank you for helping me book so many speaking engagements, and for your friendship, too.

To my friend Charlie Trotter and my American mother, Candi Olander, for their generous support and encouragement.

To one of the best teachers I've ever had, my boy, David Hite, at McNaughton and Gunn Printers; Dave, thanks for being so helpful when I was printing my first book — and sorry I forgot to give you a shout-out last time. I hope this makes up for it!

To my editor, Megan Tingley, and all the wonderful folks at Little, Brown and Company — Amy Geduldig, Sara Morling, Alyssa Morris, Anne Zafian, Bill Boedeker, Allison Devlin, Alvina Ling, Michael Conathan, Saho Fujii, Christine Cuccio, and David Ford — for giving me the opportunity to write this book, and for all your hard work.

To MY Literary Agency, and my ever-supportive agent, Mary Yockey.

To the best booksellers in America, Anderson's Book Shop! Thank you for your tireless support. Thank you, as well, to all the bookstores that have supported me from the beginning.

To Stephen Covey, Zig Ziglar, and others who've greatly influenced my thinking; I hope this book adds to the great work that you've already contributed.

To the winning edge, my boy Dave Berger, thank you for your tremendous support in editing this book, and helping me with all aspects of my business — most of all though, thank you for your friendship.

To my mother and father, for instilling a powerful Code within me, and to Hntsa, Mehret, Mulu, and Tewolde, for being a priceless part of my life.

And finally to the spirit that has guided and watched me. I thank you for the life and breath you give me, and pray that you lead me in good paths, and give me the faith, hope, and love to live a mighty Code.

Men and women are limited not by the place of their birth, not by the color of their skin, but by the size of their hope.
— *John Johnson*

Twenty years from now you will be more disappointed by the things that you didn't do than by the ones you did do. So throw off the bowlines. Sail away from the safe harbor. Catch the trade winds in your sails. Explore. Dream. Discover.
— *Mark Twain*

The probability that we may fail in the struggle ought not to deter us from the support of a cause we believe to be just.
— *Abraham Lincoln*

The saddest summary of a life contains three descriptions: could have, might have, and should have.
— *Louis E. Boone*

We began by imagining that we are giving to them; we end by realizing that they have enriched us.

— *Pope John Paul II*

What lies behind us and what lies before us are tiny matters compared to what lies within us.

— *Ralph Waldo Emerson*

Our greatest fear is not that we are inadequate. Our deepest fear is that we are powerful beyond measure.

— *Marianne Williamson*

Wanting something is not enough. You must hunger for it. Your motivation must be absolutely compelling in order to overcome the obstacles that will invariably come your way.

— *Les Brown*

In great attempts it is glorious even to fail.

— *Vince Lombardi*

Alone we can do so little; together we can do so much.

— *Helen Keller*

Good ideas are not adopted automatically. They must be driven into practice with courageous patience.

— *Admiral Hyman Rickover*

We make a living by what we get, but we make a life by what we give.

— *Winston Churchill*

Whether you believe you can or believe you can't, you're probably right.

— *Henry Ford*

NEVER LOSE HOPE

If you (or people you know) are encountering difficult times, remember the 4th Secret: Never Lose Hope. You can get help and information from the people at these organizations:

National Eating Disorder Hotline	1-800-248-3285
Eating Disorder Recovery Online	www.something-fishy.org
Alateen (Alcoholics Anonymous Teen Line)	1-800-344-2666
National Council on Alcoholism and Drug Dependence	www.ncadd.org
Narcotics Anonymous	www.na.org/links-toc.htm
Pregnancy Crisis Hotline	1-800-550-4900
National STD Hotline	1-800-227-8922
National AIDS Hotline	1-800-342-AIDS (1-800-342-2437)
Teen AIDS Hotline	1-800-440-TEEN (1-800-440-8336)
National Adolescent Suicide Hotline	1-800-SUICIDE (1-800-784-2433)

National Domestic Violence Hotline	1-800-799-SAFE (1-800-799-7233)
	www.domesticviolence.com
Rape, Abuse, and Incest National Network	1-800-656-4673
Child Abuse and Neglect Hotline	1-800-842-2288
National Runaway Hotline	1-800-621-4000
Swirl — Mixed Race Community	www.swirlinc.org

GIVE FIRST, RECEIVE SECOND

Want to follow through on the 3rd Secret? You can contribute to your community through lots of groups; here are a few with a national reach:

United Way	national.unitedway.org/myuw
VolunteerMatch	www.volunteermatch.org
America's Charities	1-800-458-9505
	www.charities.org

Called "Magnetic" by Harvard Magazine and "Amazing" by Oprah Winfrey, Mawi Asgedom has inspired hundreds of thousands of people with his leadership principles, personal story, and energy. His clients range from middle schools and high schools to colleges, community groups, and Fortune 500 companies, including:

Bank of America	Highland Park (Ill.) Schools
Boston Public Schools	Miami (Ohio) University
Chicago Public Schools	Naperville (Ill.) Schools
Delta Upsilon International Fraternity	Rotary International
Deloitte and Touche	

"From the moment Mawi began until he ended, the students were glued to the stage and his words. Many took notes. No one left. No one. In my eleven years here, I've never seen such a reception for a speaker. He'll be quite an inspiration for your students."
— Barbara McClure, English Department Chair, Santa Rosa Junior College, Santa Rosa, California.

"Mawi's inspiring presentation and his Higher Standards journal both gave Bank of America's Brand and Advertising Group fantastic strategies for personal leadership. I've encouraged other departments to hire him, and I'd recommend Mawi to any company, anywhere."
— Todd Decker, Brand & Advertising executive, Bank of America

"Mawi Asgedom is a speaker that your group will not soon forget . . . I have seen him present at civic clubs, middle schools, high schools, and churches . . . (his) dynamism, his heartfelt delivery, and his captivating story make him a topnotch and highly unique storyteller. Your audience will be fortunate to hear another as inspirational as Mawi."
— Ed Porter, President, Oklahoma City Rotary Club

"Countless numbers of students and staff have thanked me for inviting [Mawi] to our school. [He has] had a profound impact on people who [he] will never have an opportunity to meet."
— Greg Fantozzi, Ph.D., Principal, Geneva High School, Geneva, Illinois

"Mawi Asgedom gave one of the most successful speeches at Harvard Commencement in 1999 that I have heard in the 21 years I have been coaching the speakers. He is witty and personable, the kind of speaker one likes the moment he begins to talk, and he is able in simple and elegant language to convey profound truth with brevity and sincerity. He would be ideal in speaking to students, whether in high school or college, on subjects close to his head and his heart."
— Richard Marius, Retired Senior Lecturer, Harvard University

To learn more about Mawi's speaking services, and to receive his free inspirational e-newsletter, please visit www.mawispeaks. com or send e-mail to info@mawispeaks.com.

LEAD YOURSELF EVERY DAY
With Mawi's *Win the Inner Battle* Journal

You've learned about the power of The Code. Now you can make sure you live out your Code with *Win the Inner Battle: The Ultimate Teen Leadership Journal.*

In just five minutes a day, *Win the Inner Battle* will help you choose your inner and outer goals and incorporate them into your life. That way, you won't just Win the Inner Battle once, you'll Win Every Day.

Over 5 weeks, you'll learn how to:
- Build a more effective Code;
- Make your Code a regular part of your life;
- Check how well you're living up to your Code;
- Take yourself higher than ever before.

Win the Inner Battle is ideal for:
- **Teens** who want to lead themselves;
- **High schools and middle schools** seeking leadership training or character education for their student body.

For more information, visit **www.mawispeaks.com**
For use in schools, e-mail **journal@mawispeaks.com**